How Triathlon Ruined My Life

HOW TRIATHLON RUINED MY LIFE

Copyright © Darren Roberts 2007

ISBN 978-184426-469-8

First published 2007 by
UPFRONT PUBLISHING LTD
Peterborough, England.

Printed by Printondemand-Worldwide Ltd.

How Triathlon Ruined My Life

by

Darren Roberts

'...Ironman is like doing a parachute jump, whatever happens you are going to hit the ground. It's just a question of how hard...'

Darren Roberts 2006

Acknowledgements

I'd like to thank myself mainly, for putting myself through torture that is Ironman and the extraordinary amount of time, effort and money I spent doing so. Also, my long suffering wife who had to bring our daughter up single-handedly whilst I maintained a healthy relationship with everything triathlon related.

I'd like to show my appreciation to the sport of triathlon for completely taking over my life in every way and making me stare at my training schedules as if looking into a crystal ball seeking the answer to the meaning of life.

To all the people I kicked and punched in swim starts – I apologise. To the people that hit me, I'll get you next time....

Coach Kiddle, having blasted hundreds of pounds his way for his illegible training programmes, the periodisation of which I never did work out in the end. Without those schedules I would've undoubtedly over-trained and done too much too soon. He also had all the small practical tips that were invaluable, which you can only get from

someone who's been there, done it and got the t-shirt......
Kiddle I salute you.

To all the myopic car and white van drivers, what goes
around comes around....

Extra thanks to (in no particular order)

Mark at Science in Sport - www.scienceinsport.com
Stuart at Oxyshot – www.puralife.co.uk
Neal at Red Bull – www.redbull.co.uk
Jon and Daz at Pro Athlete Supplementation – www.p-a-s.biz
Jon at Think Fitness – www.thinkfitness.net
Rufus – www.rufuscrosby.com
Martyn at SBR Sports – www.sbrsports.com
Mike at Bridgtown Cycles – www.btownbikes.com
Rick at Rick Kiddle Coaching – www.rickkiddle.com
Nick at F2K – www.f2kmultisports.co.uk
220 Magazine – www.220triathlon.co.uk
John at Tri and Run – www.triandrun.com

▍Foreword

When getting into triathlon I scoured the book shops and the internet looking for information on Ironman, anything and everything was looked at. But it was all too scientific for me, which may sound strange given my profession. There wasn't anything out there about what it was actually like to train and complete an Ironman from a personal point of view.

I was convinced this 'human' story would bring up all the small details that the training manuals didn't. So I decided I'd write my own personal story in my own way, which in turn might give someone a small tip or helpful hint for the big day. Which is highly unlikely given the fact I can't write and have never written a book before, so it will be amazing if anyone can make any sense of anything.

I'd never run farther than a half marathon and in the years since running them had ballooned in size and weight due to my comprehensive weight training sessions. I hadn't ridden a bike since I was 15, and that was a BMX. I couldn't do more than 25m of crawl without stopping and gasping for breath.

Despite this I convinced myself I could go from that starting point to finishing an Ironman in 6 months, which would be just 3 months after my first ever triathlon, thinking my vocational knowledge would give me an advantage. It didn't. I discovered that it doesn't matter who you are, what you are or what you may already know – Ironman is so completely different, the 'theory' tends to break down when you get into it. Ironman is a great leveller, both physically and mentally.

The impact on my home and work life was massive when training for Ironman, so much so that I admitted had I known how much was actually involved I probably wouldn't have gone straight into doing a full Ironman – but I did have my reasons which I explain in this book.

I hope you enjoy this book. I hope you do pick up some useful tips, or maybe confirm what you already know. Even if it's just to ease that overwhelming feeling of anxiety you seem to permanently have that no matter what training you do, it's never enough. Besides, there's always someone worse off than you…!

If you don't enjoy this book, or think it's crap, then frankly I don't care! I shall be 'dining out' on this book for as long as possible and no doubt will have an enforced 'don't bring that book with you…' when invited to dinner parties. That sentence in itself suggests I'm cultured and house trained by presuming I get invited to dinner parties in the first place. Which I don't.

Take it for what it is and read it as a triathlete, written by someone pretending to be a triathlete, not as a literary critic for 'The Times'. Unless of course you are a literary critic for 'The Times', in which case….shall I shut up now? OK.

Chapter 1

Moments of clarity

What is a moment of clarity? Have you ever really had a moment of clarity? Because if you haven't, you're in for a real treat. I'm lucky to have had several moments of clarity in my life, and believe me you'll know when you're having one. The question is, what do you do with them? Being a moment of clarity the answer is usually obvious, as is the course of action to take. For example;

Whilst serving in the forces (1989-1998), we were deployed on exercise somewhere in England. We'd established ourselves on a disused WWII airfield which was then used for Helicopter Ops. Our job was to protect the choppers. Being a WWII airfield it had a traditional two storey flat roofed building for a control tower ideal for setting up some sort of OP (observation post). Unfortunately it had a large amount of standing water on the roof, so we were duly instructed to remove said standing water. However, the reason there was a large amount of standing water was because;

a) The roof was flat

b) It was pissing down

So there we were, sweeping water off a flat roof, in torrential rain. It wasn't quite as bad as sweeping leaves in the wind but as an exercise in pointlessness it was close. The answer was obvious, it was time to leave. Which I did two years later, however that wasn't until after I'd had a head on encounter with an Astra-van whilst out on my GSXR-600, which resulted in two operations, nine pins and two metal plates. Thankfully, I remember nothing of the accident as I was knocked unconscious straight away and didn't regain consciousness, until some time later in the ambulance, where I noticed my left arm was pointing in several different directions. The unfortunate thing about the whole episode was that whilst lying in the road drifting in and out of consciousness, I announced to the crowd that had gathered round my crumpled body, that 'my parachute didn't open…'; something that was relayed to me by the police whilst in hospital. That was 1997.

My Ironman moment of clarity came 55 miles into the 112 mile bike course with my legs burning, realising I had to tackle over 6000ft of climbing over three laps followed by running a marathon – having never run a marathon before. I'd joked during the months leading up to the Ironman that the question 'why?' would be one I'd be asking myself many times on the day – but that wasn't the case. The question 'why?' was one I tortured myself with on a daily basis, usually before speaking a sentence along the lines of;

'I'm going out on my bike,' wife upstairs with baby replies. 'How long are you out for?'

'Six hours, then I'm off on a 2hr run...' Why? Why? Why?

You see, by entering an Ironman you set something in motion which can't be stopped. I felt a little bit like the lookout on '*Titanic*', 'loooook out captain! Ironman ahead!' This isn't a 10km run or a half marathon you jog around with your friends dressed as a polar bear or wearing a charity t-shirt. You can't just knock a few sessions out in the weeks before and bluff it on the day – no sireeeeeee bob. People do, and they're the ones talking to themselves at feed stations, or you see their bikes propped up against the ambulances along the route. Unlike anything you've done before, training for Ironman isn't really 'optional'. Ironman is like parachuting from a plane – whatever happens you're going to hit the ground, it's just a case of how hard.

There's lots of different things snipping away at the cords of that parachute. Wife 'snip', kids 'snip', work 'snip', having some sort of life 'snip snip snip'. The efficacy of that parachute is rapidly diminishing; this is going to hurt........

So you see, my moment of clarity 55 miles into the bike on race day was a little late. That was 2006.

Chapter 2

The beginning was the end……

My Ironman journey had actually started a long time ago. I'd watched a documentary on Discovery Channel, or something similar, not long after leaving the forces. I knew what triathlon was, and I appreciated what seemed to be the superhuman effort required to complete the IM distance, having watched people wobble across the line in pitch dark with day-glo sticks stuck to their backs like mad night-clubbers. Although I suspected they were not having quite as good a time as people taking recreational drugs in a club think they are, or were they?

I was a muscle monkey and had been for years, the aerobic fitness required to complete a feat such as Ironman would mean a drastic reduction in size. Plus, I had the swimming ability of a bus - not good for the 2.4 mile swim - or any swim for that matter, unless by *'swimming'* it meant running and *'bombing'* people in a pool which I was very good at. Since leaving the forces, and with un-interrupted access to a gym and decent food (no pesky roof rain sweeping episodes or 6 month trips to Bosnia etc) I'd ballooned to 100kgs and was able to bench press small houses. However, my aerobic exercise consisted of breathing in and out. I was also what I call 'reverse-anorexic', like most people who train big I was convinced I was shrinking when not in the gym or eating. A missed session or protein drink could spell disaster psychological-ly as I imagined muscles atrophying – even though I knew this not to be the case. However, training had also become a chore. The sets and reps were automatic; the gains tiny.

My training had gone from a traditional split to one body part per day, then to major muscle groups in one go. Work meant I couldn't commit to five weight sessions per week (chest at 8pm at night with no-one to spot me didn't float my boat), so I'd cut it back to bench, pull-ups and dead-lifts in a 15RM circuit. I was hitting all the big muscles and by doing 15RM in a circuit was building some muscular endurance back in. Every now and again I'd chuck a 5RM workout in along with doing guns (arms) on their own. I enjoyed this for a while, but soon my enthusiasm started to drop again and it was back to simply being a boring part of my life. What was wrong? This was more than your usual loss of interest - I realised I'd been doing weights for 13 years and it was time for a change. A big change, a very big change.

By this time I'd talked my way into the job of Head of Strength & Conditioning at energy drink Red Bull, after a three year stint as a personal trainer. My lack of 'fitness' began to play on my mind as I came into contact with elite endurance-based athletes through Red Bull. I could chuck the same weight around as the rugby boys and sprinters, but what did I really know about endurance performance other than the theory? Hmmmmmmm. I thrived on practical application and self experimentation, but puffing round the Manchester 10km every year fuelled on caffeine wasn't giving me the first hand insight I needed to the endurance athlete. Through Red Bull I'd met a guy called Rick Kiddle – he was British Triathlon Champion in 1989 and had also finished a few Ironman races, including Hawaii. It sounded incredible. Despite being 300 years old, and now having knees made of soft cheese, his enthusiasm for the sport was infectious. After talking to him something was nagging in my head about this event, but I couldn't put my finger on it. At a leisure industry show one of the instructors was training for an Ironman – I looked in awe, but he was a dweeb! He had a bandana on! And a pony tail!! This is 2004, not 1994! It was there that a serious seed was sown. If someone could train for an Ironman who wore a pony tail *AND* a bandana – then why couldn't I?

I was no stranger to physically arduous things. Twelve years previously I'd had to pass pre-para selection to join the Parachute Squadron of the RAF Regiment. Three weeks of physical and mental hell - so surely I was capable of training for an Ironman?

The aim of Pre-Para is to weed out who is fit enough to earn their para wings, but in reality it is a war of physical attrition with a 60% failure rate. It wasn't about who was *'fit enough'* but who could get through it either injury free or with injuries you could cope with, usually involving eating anti-inflammatory pills like smarties. Gym tests followed immediately by a bleep test, followed immediately by a BFT (battle fitness test), followed by the assault course four times followed by a five mile cross country run – and that was just the first morning. The three weeks went along in that vein, apart from a week long stint being beasted around the Grampian Mountains in

Scotland. At the end of the course there were just eight of us left out of forty five that had started – with some seriously destroyed knees, backs etc. So if I'd done that, surely I had the mentality to cope with training for an Ironman?

Months slipped past with stuff like buying a flat and getting married. Moving into the new flat was another shift in gears for me – just one year previously I'd been moaning about the fact that the only thing I possessed was CD's, DVD's and clothes. Here I was one year later with a mortgage, a car and moving in with my girlfriend. I'd bought the flat from a former personal training client when the building was just a shell. They were property investors and had bought a number of the apartments, including one for me. I was expecting a tiny place on the ground floor with the budget I had, but when the plans arrived I discovered my flat was on the top floor facing the newly developed Marina. Result!

It was a derelict brick warehouse and as usual with these sorts of things the completion of the building was all behind schedule. We managed to get in before Christmas 2003 and get settled. We'd also booked a holiday to California over Christmas and New Year. It was going to be Amy's first time over there. I'd spent a lot of time in California, I love the place and take every opportunity to go back to Laguna Beach. The trip involved showing Amy all there was to see in Southern California, Hollywood - which is a dump, but I had to show Amy just how crap it actually is - Universal Studios, tour the stars houses, go to Vegas and get married, go to Laguna Beach to stay with my friends. Yes, I did just say get married in Vegas, although Amy didn't know that was the plan at the time.

After arriving in California, we spent the first few days in

The beginning was the end......

Hollywood and Universal studios. Amy loved it! From there we left for our four day trip to Vegas, which included New Year's Eve. I'd already had the wedding rings specially made in Manchester. I wasn't sure what the crack was with getting married over there and spent hours researching on the internet. Basically, you have to go to the county court house in downtown Vegas pay $50 for a marriage licence (you both have to be present) and it's open 24 hours a day, 7 days a week (obviously, this is *Vegas baby*). As for somewhere to get married in Vegas, the sky's the limit but if you're going to get married in Vegas there's only one way to do it – ELVIS STYLEEE! We'd talked about getting married, and we had both agreed that when the time came we'd go away and tie the knot. Amy's dad had sadly died years before, and I've never been into the idea of paying for a huge wedding, which is ultimately paying for a three course meal for a load of people you hardly know, and who don't like each other anyway.

Vegas blew Amy away. I'd already been a few times and it's somewhere that's impossible to get bored of or used to. We were there for four days which is about as much as you can take in one go. If you haven't been to Vegas you must go, it's one of those places you must visit before you die. It was the last place I thought I'd enjoy, but it's hilarious. It's difficult to describe – it's a cartoon made real in the middle of the desert. We were staying in the 'Excalibur' hotel which is the medieval themed hotel. Most of the hotels have a theme and are absolutely enormous. Sadly, the quality and opulence of the hotels mean that when you come home and stay in hotels in the UK, they all look crap, even the 5 star ones.

I did a recce on the wedding sketch and discovered that the only place in Vegas that did an Elvis wedding was the

'*Graceland Wedding Chapel*'. Now all we had to do was get a marriage licence, but how did I go about it as a surprise when both of us had to be present to apply for one? After some really obscure persuading, Amy thought we were just going down for the laugh and getting a marriage licence for the crack. With marriage licence in hand we headed back to the hotel. Amy went back to the room while she thought I was wandering around the shops. What I was actually doing was booking our wedding - 7pm on the 31st December. The limo would pick us up outside the hotel at 6.30pm. As an insurance policy I'd texted everyone I knew before getting on the plane at Manchester airport telling them what I had planned – that way I couldn't back out……

We got dressed up ready for the New Year celebrations in Vegas, which are HUGE. The wedding was at the perfect time as the main strip gets closed down after 9pm. We headed out to the front of the hotel, and sure enough at 6.30pm the limo rocked up! Amy had no clue what was going on and it was only when in the limo en route did I 'fess up'. I didn't actually *ask* Amy to marry me. We were already in the limo on the way to the chapel, I'd already booked the wedding, and simply produced the rings I'd had made back in Manchester out of my back pocket! I think she was in shock – so like all good predators I moved in for the kill while she was still stunned.

We arrived at the place and it was hilarious, it stank of mould and was in a really dodgy part of town in a long road of equally dodgy wedding chapels. We didn't know it at the time but just two chapels down the road Britney Spears was getting married at the *Little White Wedding Chapel*. Thankfully, our marriage has lasted a bit longer. Once in the place the comedy just got better – it was like being in a *'Blackpool Beach meets Hollywood nightmare'*. It was 'tacky-ness' that cheesy seaside towns can only dream of. The bouquets of flowers were, in fact, plastic, had gone grey and had in inch of dust on them. We weren't allowed to use our own camera and had to buy one of theirs – a *'Graceland Wedding Chapel'* own brand disposable. I paid the guy behind the desk $10 to be our photographer for the evening. We were talked through the ceremony and had a quick look at the 'Chapel', basically a small wooden building with a reception area (which is where the bride waited), which was also the entrance to the place. The 'chapel' itself was just a room with seats in that stank of mould.

Elvis didn't actually do the ceremony, that was done by some dodgy Puerto-Rican dude with tattoos all over his neck and hands. They were full on gangster tattoos. Anyone can 'marry' someone over there. You just have to register and get a licence, you don't have to be a collar wearing member of the God squad. This guy had clearly decided to be a 'minister' once being released from prison after serving his 20 years for murdering his sister's boyfriend or something. Elvis' job was to give the bride away and sing his songs as we tied the knot.

I positioned myself at the front of the chapel with Elvis strumming his guitar. It was all a bit of a rush as they had back to back weddings all night – as with everything in Vegas it's 24 hours a day 7 days a week. Elvis went to get Amy, who was stood in reception, but as they walked back through the door someone realised that the battered 10 year old boom box that played the wedding music wasn't on and the hammered wedding tape hadn't been rewound from the service 10 minutes before! The 'minister' rewound the tape and pressed play which was Amy and Elvis's cue to come back in, except they didn't. As I found out from Amy later, the woman behind the reception desk was gesturing frantically to Amy and Elvis to go through the doors whilst booking another wedding in on the phone. She kindly kicked the door open with her foot and held it there, whilst keeping the phone to her ear. This was perfect! You couldn't make this stuff up. I noticed they'd let Amy have one of the discoloured grey plastic bouquets.

Amy walked down the 'aisle' with 'Elvis'. We duly carried out the ceremony with our photographer snapping and re-winding away at the disposable. It was hard to keep a straight face and in some of the photo's I couldn't help assuming an 'Elvis' pose. Soon enough we were done and married! The comedy and surreal nature of the whole thing meant it didn't actually sink in. We walked out of the place and into the limo, which took us back to the hotel. It was a very bizarre situation, but very 'Vegas'. I also realised at this point I hadn't told my mum or Amy's mum, They weren't recipients of my text insurance before leaving Manchester airport. We got back to the hotel and enjoyed the rest of the NYE celebrations, which consisted of the biggest firework display you'll ever see in your life. The next morning I awoke next to my wife (!), and we set off to see if anywhere was open to get the wedding pictures developed. Why we thought this might not be possible with it being New Year's Day, I have no idea – this was Vegas so it didn't matter whether it was Christmas day, New Years day, or a Wednesday in March, as everything was open. We handed the pictures in and floated around for an hour. When we picked them up they didn't disappoint. The best way to describe them was – the guy was taking pictures of the place, and we got in the way! Again, you couldn't have planned or made this stuff up. We nearly pissed ourselves laughing. It was exactly the story we wanted for our kids.

The beginning was the end......

Your wedding day is supposed to be memorable, right? This was!

When we got back to the UK, things were different and I don't mean because I was married. I was completely fed up with doing weights and the thought of getting back into the gym to lift made me roll my eyes. If I was bored of them before, I now resented going to the gym to do them – it had to be replaced with something more fulfilling.....

Chapter 3

You never jump, you're pushed

The Ironman seed was growing. I couldn't swim crawl very well (just how bad was to become apparent in Maidenhead Leisure Centre in November 2005), and I was maxed out with work. As 2004 went by I began openly discussing with people about maybe taking triathlon up and sacking off the weights etc, etc. I even began talking about Ironman, but in reality it was so far away from what I was capable of even I didn't really believe I was ever going to *actually* do one. I knew that anyone who talked to me at the time was just agreeing with me in that friendly way people do, i.e. you're talking bollocks. I was probably going to train for one in one way or another and maybe even do some Olympic distance races, but was I actually going to do an Ironman? For some reason though, Ironman wouldn't go away.

Early in 2005 I called Rick Kiddle, who I hadn't seen or spoken to for at least 18 months, and tortured him for information about taking up triathlon - the do's and don'ts from a former pro. For Rick this was another random phone call from someone who in all probability wouldn't actually do a triathlon, let alone an Ironman. I explained that the 13 year love affair with weights was coming to an end, and it was time for a change. Rick duly gave me all the advice I needed. I did nothing, well not exactly nothing. Amy was expecting our first child, so I was wrapped up in that, as you would be.

As always, work was becoming increasingly busy. I'd be at a British Superbike race with Red Bull Honda at the weekend; come home Sunday night to fly to a European Tour golf event in Europe on Monday; fly back in time for meetings, and briefly say hello to Amy before disappearing again. I'm not complaining. I love my job and was getting paid to work with some of the best sportspeople in the world. During my time with Red Bull I'd worked with, and become friends with, household names. It wasn't really a 'job', I was living the dream. My incompetence had also continued to go unnoticed, and to the amazement of my former work colleagues in the forces, I was still in a job. Even so, the months flew by as I was so busy and, having not done anything about getting into triathlon, I carried on brainlessly lifting weights. Then, in August 2005 two things happened that changed me.

Firstly, my daughter Lilly-Mae was born. As anyone who's a parent knows, when the little dude arrives, you change. You start to re-assess what you've done, how you've done it, and what legacy you are leaving behind. What impression on the world will you leave, if any? All these possibilities of the person I could have been, which had narrowed down with every passing year, suddenly evaporated to one when Lilly-Mae was born. I was the person I was going to be, and now it was *for real* as I had a tiny life to look out for. Everything took on a new dimension. Even though I thought I had a good handle on life, having spent nine years in the military travelling the world and now being responsible for elite athletes, I couldn't help looking at things differently.

Ironman seemed like something I *had* to do, not talk about. Since when did I talk about things and not *actually* do them? I could see the conversation with my daughter:

'I was going to do an Ironman, but never got round to it.'

'Eh? What, Dad? Never got round to it? It was doing an Ironman, not calling your mum to see if she wanted to come round for tea! How could you *not get round to it*?'

Another call was placed to the Kiddle in his nursing home. More knowledge was imparted, and now I really had to do something. It was becoming embarrassing. Why was I even continuing to think about it or talk about it? Just enter one, you idiot! The plan was do Half Ironman UK (or Ironman 70.3 as it's now known) in June 2006 followed by the big one in August 2007. That gave me eighteen months to train. Plenty of time. Having decided on my triathlon strategy all I needed to do now was actually enter. I'd got the green light from Amy (who, like France in the UN Security Council, has veto power on all decisions), having convinced her it would be a cheap sport to get in to (oh the naivety). But the new baby and work stalled the actual 'entering'. But you never jump do you? You're pushed.

The second thing to happen was one of the young Red Bull athletes I worked with was killed in a race. I'm not really sure what to write about this. I think the easiest thing is to simply put down what I wrote immediately after his death and sent straight to the editor of 'Motorcycle Racer', Larry

Carter. Lazza knows me anyway as I used to write for the mag, and he's the 'voice' of the BSB paddock at every round.

'...Words of comfort or trying to rationalise about this tragedy are pointless. Where I find solace is thinking about Chris's talent, which was beyond question and Red Bull Honda were lucky to have the luxury of being able to select him for the Rookies programme. I had no doubt that I would be watching him in GP's in a few years and sending him abusive text messages as he would have binned us all off to relax in his motor home with his supermodel girlfriend.

It was my job to patch him back together after an off (which they were plenty of at the beginning of the season!), and Cadwell was no different as I had him covered in all sorts of tape and ice packs. Watching him disappear in a cloud of two stroke towards the grid, it wasn't in the front of my mind that would be the last time I saw him – and it shouldn't have. Chris was living his dream and was going all the way, there's no time to think about what might happen in a race apart from getting a podium.

I'm just extremely fortunate to be able to say I worked with the kid, and he'll live on racing bikes in my heart. He gave me his bottle of champagne from his 2nd place at Silverstone to celebrate the birth of my daughter Lilly-Mae 6 days previously, and when she's old enough I'll be able to tell her all about him...'

Now I'm a big boy, and when it comes to life and the shit it can throw at you, I like to think I'm fairly pragmatic about it. I'd had several friends killed in the forces and even during my time with Red Bull another one of our young riders, Guy Farbrother, was killed in a road traffic accident at just 18 years old in 2003, the day after a race. Just a few days previously he'd been training with me in Manchester, so I was no stranger to tragedy and young lives being cut short. I'd stopped trying to rationalise such deaths because you couldn't, life was just being a bitch in the worst possible way.

It was a tough, tough time. Being a new parent suddenly made this all different. My pragmatic attitude towards death and tragedy evaporated. Amy saw me cry for the first time in three years of being together, when I found out that Chris's life support machine had been turned off the day after the race. I couldn't believe he was actually dead; if I felt like this then what did his parents feel like? How would I feel if it were Lilly-Mae? I'd got off on the wrong foot with Chris's dad when we first met, and that was one of the many things that preyed on my mind after Chris was killed. We'd got on fine eventually and there was no problem, but that initial friction seemed so wasteful. I was angry with myself for it. Had I played a part in Chris's death? Was he really fit to ride? The answer of course was I played no part in his death, no-one had. It was a tragic racing accident – no logic, no mercy.

The funeral was horrendous. It was heart breaking on an unimaginable scale, such a young life and talent cut down. But he was doing something he loved, he was living his dream - Clive and Pam did everything they could to help him live that dream. As parents you're never going to knowingly put your child in danger, and what are you going to do anyway? Wrap them in cotton wool and never let them leave the house? Someone once told me living was the only thing worth dying for, and Chris had squeezed more into his fourteen years than most of us do in a lifetime.

We all like to think we live life to the full. Live for today and don't save it for tomorrow because, well, there might not be a tomorrow. Truth is, very few of us live like that and despite the tragic deaths of those around me over the years, I'd slipped into the work grind. If you watch documentaries with survivors of plane crashes and ferry accidents etc, they all talk about how they truly live for the moment, having stared death in the face. I'd nearly been killed several times during my time in the forces, and I mean *nearly* killed but I'd forgotten all about that and gotten bogged down in *life.* Don't get me wrong, my current job isn't actually a 'job', and there isn't a day goes by where I'm not grateful for what I've got, but still, I was so preoccupied with providing for my new family I was slipping down that slope.

The aftermath of Chris's death for me was a paradigm shift in outlook on life – if people thought I was living a full life before, all the stops had come out for definite now. If I didn't want to train, I didn't. If I wanted some sweets, I ate them. If I fancied a beer in the evening, I had one. I basically began living life as I wanted to. I binned off all the little rules that existed in my life. I also went straight online to Ironman UK, got the credit card out, and entered for the FULL Ironman in August 2006. Bollocks to pissing about with my eighteen month training plan – just do the full Charlie and stop messing about! So I did.

Chapter 4

Let the comedy begin

A couple of days after entering, I called coach Kiddle (he was just having his urine soaked tartan blanket changed by his nurse), told him I'd entered the big daddy and asked him if nine months was long enough to train for it. He seemed confident it was possible. He'd trained plenty of people from triathlon virgins to Ironman before. We booked a day and time for me to go to his place and undergo some triathlon specific fitness testing. It was a four hour drive from Manchester but this was Ironman, this was serious. A good friend of mine had expressed an interest in triathlon and had set himself the goal of completing an Olympic distance event in the summer of 2006. The 'Rickster' was a fountain of great ideas that ended up falling by the wayside. His heart was in the right place but inevitably the weekend got in the way, along with the partying that went with it. Being long haul cabin crew, and actually *straight,* meant anything and everything was on a plate for him.

Unfortunately, his penchant for hard partying and psychotic women meant all his energy was taken up by exactly that. We'd shared a flat for almost two years before moving out, as we'd both bought places. He was moving in with his total bunny boiling (now ex) girlfriend, and I was moving in with Amy. Getting into triathlon was Rick's way of giving himself something to do that was healthy, instead of going on a bender with a load of bang-up-for-it air hostesses, or trying to cope with whatever lunatic he was dating. When he got to whatever country he happened to be in he had something to train for. I wasn't about to let this be yet another great idea that fell by the wayside, so I duly bullied him into coming with me for the fitness testing. If I was going to do Ironman then he was going to do the Olympic Dsitance race – simple as.

The day of the fitness testing arrived. It was a 6am start from Manchvegas and we drove down to see coach Kiddle. We rocked up to Kiddle's place, and I won't bore you with the details but I was in good shape (as I should be) but with the flexibility of someone Kiddle's age and weighing in at 94kgs. Not really Ironman weight. How many 15st Ironman triathletes do you see under 6ft? Kiddle left me with no illusions about the weight loss I had in front of me. We didn't do anything I couldn't have done myself in terms of testing, but I'd decided to use Kiddle as a coach as he's obviously got tonnes of practical experience training triathletes and it would have been stupid not to. I'm not saying you need to break the bank and retain someone to train you. However, if there's advice available, take it from someone who knows what they're talking about from experience, as it will prove invaluable. The main thing for me was the swim and bike assessments. Think about it, when was the last time you actually rode a bike? I mean *really rode a bike*, not the knackered mountain bike you got for £49.99 from Halfords that you briefly used to go to work and back on, but *really* rode one?

We left for SBR Sports (Swim, Bike, Run triathlon shop) in Windsor to look at some bikes and take them for a spin, this also doubled as the bike assessment. Rick and I looked like complete idiots on the bikes, running tights, fleeces and running trainers – Jesus it makes me cringe to look back on that now. We were on LeMonde Reno's, a very reasonable bike that at £700 which would do everything I wanted it to. Obviously you could spend £1000's on a bike but what would be the point in that? (Take note of this for late...) I was just starting out and needed something that would get the job done. We bombed off on the bikes and were spectacularly crap, crunching gears, poor position - it was a mess.

After that debacle, we left for Maidenhead swimming pool for the swim assessment. This was my Achilles heel (and is most triathletes Achilles heel), I was not looking forward to it in any way. Looking back knowing what I know now, had I seen myself swimming that day I would have laughed out loud at the suggestion this person was going to swim 2.4 miles in a lake, in nine months' time. Ignorance is bliss. To be fair Kiddle was encouraging, said we weren't the worst he'd seen and he'd coached someone from a non swimmer to Ironman in six months, so at least I could 'swim' – which for the time being involved flapping arms wildly like a dolphin in distress having got lost in the Bristol Channel. It took me 32 strokes to cover 25m which, if you don't know, is bobbins and at the end of that 25m I had a purple face. Richard, my ex-flatmate, displayed early promise and flair in the pool, great – even my chain-smoking, hard-partying buddy was better than me at swimming. Where's the weights room again?

After a long day, we headed back up the M6 to Manchester discussing the days events – the Ironman journey had started for me. I didn't know it at the time, but my life as I knew it was essentially over……..

Chapter 5

Like all addictions, it starts small...

My monthly training programme arrived from Kiddle a couple of days after the testing. My plan was to get a few schedules from him, then using my own professional knowledge and experience, start writing my own. At £80 a time I wasn't going to keep getting them from him for the next nine months. (Excuse me while I laugh out loud at my naivety).

All my different heart rate zones had been worked out. Using *220* minus your age is a crap way, as everyone is different and your HR values can vary daily. I had five different zones, ranging from easy to eye bleeding, with the values being slightly different, depending on whether it was swimming, biking or running. Typically, running generates the highest values, followed by biking, then swimming. This means the HR you work at to achieve the same intensity varies, depending on the discipline. Over time, the difference between bike and run HR values narrows, as you get fitter.

This is why it's advisable to get some sort of professional advice before tackling something as stupid as Ironman. You don't want your Ironman journey to end in a feed station, talking to yourself, do you? Most decent triathlon clubs can help with this for a fraction of the cost I was paying Kiddle, and I'll go into my triathlon club experience shortly, but me being me, I wanted the best, so was happy to pay the wedge to coach Kiddle. Besides I was going to have to lay out for all the kit I needed anyway, so a few extra quid on coaching wasn't going to break the bank, was it?

I also sorted out the triathlon package from SBR, which was the first time I actually sat down and went through what I needed. SBR, like most triathlon shops, do packages where you can buy the bulk of the main items you need at a discount. Obviously I hadn't even thought about what I really needed or what it cost, but that didn't stop me telling the wife it wouldn't be much. As to exactly what it would cost, we'll get to that later.....

Bike

My trusty LeMonde Reno. The very bike I test rode with such spectacular inefficiency, I named 'Renny'. I was to spend many, many hours on this bike and it's still going strong now.

Wetsuit

An end of season 'Ironman Instinct' wetsuit which was half-price, I felt a bit of a tit wearing something Ironman branded, as I actually hadn't done an Ironman yet.

Like all addictions, it starts small...

Peddles

Because the bike doesn't come with them. Why would it?

Shoes

These clip into the peddles and take some getting used to, especially when stopping at traffic lights.

Tri suit

A one-piece, crowd-pleasing, lycra race suit.

Helmet

Amazingly, these things cost a fortune, but keep the noggin in one piece.

Turbo trainer

Vital for winter training, and something I was to grow to hate very shortly.

Tool kit

Spare inner tubes (when was the last time you changed a tyre on a bike!?!). Co2 canister - an amazing invention since I last rode a bike - a tiny, pressurised canister that instantly pumps your tyre up to 120psi. This makes sense, as you don't want to be fannying around with a traditional pump on Ironman, whilst crying for mummy as everyone flies past you, laughing. Which they don't, obviously, but you know what I mean.

I managed to get the whole lot for less than a grand, with

the Rickster buying exactly the same. Unfortunately, I was under the impression I had everything I needed. Jesus, I was so clueless.

I drove back down to Windsor from Manchester with the Rickster to pick all the gear up, and with the car loaded we drove all the way back up the M6. I couldn't wait to get out on the bike, I had everything I needed for a triathlon (ha!). When I arrived home with all the gear, Amy was very supportive and amazed I'd only spent £1000 - she was expecting it to be double. With everything unloaded into the flat, I was one step nearer becoming a *'triathlete'*.

It was 1st Dec and I had a one hour bike session to do at an easy pace. It was to be my *'first time'* with Renny, and like all *'first times'* you want it to be special. But the reality of *'first times'* is that they're bungling attempts by ham-fisted, inexperienced idiots. I didn't have any cycling-specific clothing – apart from shoes and helmet. I'd got a thermal Nike scull cap to wear under my helmet to keep the old cone warm, as it was FREEZING outside. I pulled on the Nike running tights - who needs cycling bottoms with their arse-saving padding? Who needs nice cycling tops with plenty of handy pockets to put stuff in? No - what you need is a Nike fleece with your mobile/wallet/house keys etc in the pockets digging into your stomach when on the bike. It's also better if the fleece is grey in colour and difficult for car drivers to see, as opposed to being some sort of high visibility colour such as, say, luminous yellow. You'd only need that if you lived in a country where drivers are so myopic and cyclist-unaware, they wouldn't see you even if you were on fire, with a big, neon, flashing sign above you saying *'cyclist on fire'*.

So there I was, wearing running gear, with my Nike scull

cap on, which made my cycling helmet sit four miles higher on my head than it was supposed to. Undeterred, I grabbed Renny and set off on my hour long ride. I was twenty minutes into the ride when I realised a number of things.

1) I had no gloves on and soon lost feeling in my hands in the freezing air, which made changing gears and braking almost impossible.

2) I had no eyewear on of any description, so that the freezing air was making my eyes water so badly I couldn't actually see.

3) Everyone was trying to run me over.

4) I was changing up gears instead of down, and vice versa.

5) I'd forgotten to put my heart rate monitor on, so had no idea how hard I was/wasn't working, nor what time it was.

It was horrible, I must've looked like some complete lunatic. Let me just remind you that I'm the Head of Strength & Conditioning at Red Bull, supposedly working with some of the best athletes in the world, and presumably knowing what I'm doing when it comes to matters of physical training. Not to mention nine years as a roughty-toughty airborne warrior. I arrived back home with a grimace, and two strings of snot frozen onto my face from the sub zero wind chill.

From that point on it was the turbo for me. The weather meant cycling outside *really* was for idiots anyway.

Besides, building a good endurance base was the priority and the turbo allowed me to train at the prescribed heart rate for a continuous time. No stop/start on the three hundred sets of traffic lights there are between where we lived in Manchester city centre and the open countryside. I got into the 'brick' training, as it's called, bike followed immediately by running, doing one hour on the turbo, then thirty minutes running. Wow! For someone who did very little aerobic training,, this was a massive step. I'm actually shaking my head writing this - if only I had known what was to come. As I keep saying, ignorance is bliss. Stop reading this book now!

I was still doing the weight circuit a couple of times per week in what was supposed to be my 'off' days. The low intensity of the triathlon programme meant I could get away with it. The low intensity was designed to build the endurance base I was going to need. The body weight plummeted, but my strength didn't. Happy days! This wasn't going to be that bad....

Kiddle had prescribed me four different types of swim. They were all drill heavy and varied from 1000m to 1500m. At the time, these seemed extremely long and took forever to complete. No-one likes swimming, apart from the people that are already good at it, which in my case was everyone apart from me. Despite being in good shape I could only complete one length of 'proper' crawl. I mean ONE LENGTH - just 25 meters. 2.4 miles loomed in front of me like Everest, but Kiddle said it was do-able. I just had to trust the professional.

With flexible working hours I could use the pool at David Lloyd when it was quiet, ensuring I had the 'fast' lane to myself as no-one else was in the pool. I worked through the swim sessions - *chicken wing, bilateral, catch-up, hypoxic* – they were crippling me. 'Swim A', which was just 1000m, was taking me nearly an hour to complete! I progressed through to 'Swim B', and whilst I was now able to at least string a massive eight lengths together without stopping, they were taking forever. When it came time to tackle the '1500m Swim C', a quick glance showed me that given the time it was taking to do the other swim sessions, this was going to be a two hour session, comprising over 160 lengths! Hang on - 160 lengths? 1500m was not 160 lengths, it was 60. What was going on?

I'll tell you what was going on, I'd completely misread what lengths to do for what drill, because Kiddle had written the programme in such a confusing way (down to being senile through old age). So for 'Swim A', which was 1000m, I was in fact covering 1500m. Instead of 1200m for Swim B, I was covering 2000m! No wonder it was taking all day to do the friggin' swims. And I'd been doing this for eight weeks! Have you ever tried doing twelve consecutive lengths of *'catch up'*, without drowning? How about *'hypoxic breathing'* for twelve straight lengths? IDIOT! I immediately rang Kiddle, who said it was my northern monkey-ness that had prevented me from reading the sessions correctly, and why hadn't I realised I was covering sixty lengths on what was supposed to be a forty length workout?

Whether it was my northern-ness or Kiddle's inability to write a legible programme from under his piss-soaked tartan blanket in his retirement home, we'll never know. But this was a blessing in disguise. The relentless hammering in the pool, doing almost twice as much as I was supposed to, had the effect of making me reasonable at swimming. So reasonable in fact, I could start going to the pool at times I *knew* other people would be there. No longer would I be in the fast lane by default, I could go in it *with other people.*

Christmas 2005 arrived and as it was Lilly-Mae's first Christmas, we stayed in the UK instead of our usual trip to California. You can't beat being on the beach on Christmas Day, but not this year. So we stayed and had our first 'family' Christmas. In the New Year my training programme marched on – as I did.

The swimming was starting to come, the running was getting better as the weight fell off and I was getting used to running 'off the bike'. I also sat down at the computer and trawled the internet for some sprint and Olympic triathlons to enter in my build up to IM, and any other events that took my fancy. First up, Wilmslow half marathon in March – I'd done this a few years ago with a time of 1hr 34mins before completely sacking the CV exercise off. I planned to beat that time. Trying to find a decent OD race was easier said than done – but the interweb pointed in the direction of Royal Windsor, Blenheim and Salford. As for a sprint distance, Eton Super Sprint announced itself as the first open water swim event of the year on closed roads. Perfect. I entered Wilmslow, Eton, Windsor and Salford. I also had Manchester 10k in May but being a mere 10km meant it didn't appear on the 'training' radar. The triathlons were all about gaining race and transition experience, something about which I'll go into detail later. I was surprised at the cost at around £60 per triathlon, but after laying out a whopping £220 for Ironman, it was all relative.

I was getting into the full flow of the training. I became intimately familiar with the turbo – and also grew to despise it. Being in the middle of winter meant I could take my turbo and bike onto the landing in the glass atrium, that housed the staircase at the side of our building. In the summer it was like a greenhouse, but in January it was like a fridge. I'd set it up, get the mp3 on and grind away. If Amy and the baby were out, I used to set it up in front of the telly with the doors open onto the Juliette balcony, my personal best being to watch *'Lord of the Rings'* from start to finish whilst on it. I was still insisting on doing these sessions wearing running tights, convinced my arse would get used to being in the saddle. It didn't.

A typical week for me at this early stage was:

Monday
Swim 1 (1000m of various intensity)
Weights

Tuesday
Bike 1hr
Stomach

Wednesday
Swim C (1500m of various drills and sprints)
2hr Bike

Thursday
Stomach/Weights
Swim 1 followed Bike 1hr

Friday
Swim 3 (1500m of yet more variations of sprints)
Bike 1hr followed by Run 20mins

Saturday
Run 1hr 10mins

Sunday
Off

I was still getting days off at this stage, and whilst I thought I was doing some healthy sessions, the real stuff was yet to come – I just didn't know it. I was also still sneaking weights sessions in when I could. I was on my third programme from Kiddle, but still hadn't worked out the progression or periodistation of it, so hadn't started doing them myself. The one thing I definitely wasn't doing was riding outside. The bike sessions were no more than two hours at this stage, so if I were to go out 1½ hours of that session would be stop/start at traffic lights, as I made my way out of the city centre and into Cheshire. So for me it was better to be on the constant resistance of the turbo, or so I thought.

The training volume increased weekly and at this stage it wasn't a problem. Work was steady, but the Superbike and Golf stuff didn't start for me until March, so I was fitting everything in (just about), including family time. Unfortunately I had no idea of just how much volume I was going to have to start doing. I'd been fitting work in and around training, as opposed to training in and around work – but this seemed completely normal to me. I'd also been fitting home life in and around training as opposed to the other way around, but I wasn't obsessed or anything. Not me. Not at all. Soon it was going to get very tough keeping my training commitments up, with work starting to get very busy, involving lots of travelling and being away from home. With it being the New Year, I decided to reacquaint myself with the my local triathlon club (which I'd actually joined) and its running track sessions.

I'd been down the club the previous summer in 2005 for a

few random track sessions, but that wasn't my first time - I'd 'dabbled' before in the summer of 2002. Someone told me that the track sessions would suit me, as they were interval based around the 600m mark and covering a total of around 5000m in the session. This did suit me, hammering it for 600m or less, followed by a short break, was something I could do and do well, despite my size at the time. I rocked up to the athletics track on a balmy summer evening, paid my £2 and hovered around. There didn't seem to be anyone there 'triathlon' orientated, just lots of kids doing footy training in the grass centre of the 400m track. Had I got the right time, right place? I could see various gaggles of people and individuals jogging around the 400m track, but these were the most random collection of people you're likely to see in one place, and triathlon was something only the uber-fit did, wasn't it? A friendly woman seeing me hovering around looking lost asked if I was OK.

'I'm here for the triathlon track session' I replied.

'That's us!' she said.

She ran the training session and advised me to jog around for a bit as a pre warm up, warm up. Yes, the odd collection of people bobbing around were the triathlon club. I jogged around, and after one lap we were called together to do the group warm up, this was my chance to size everyone up at close quarters. There were plenty of girls there, in fact more girls than guys. The guys that were there about as frosty-shouldered and unfriendly as you like, it was like being with a bunch of male silverback gorillas, with a new alpha male being introduced to the group, seriously disrupting the status-quo.

The warm up was a standard affair, but the clincher for me came when we carried out efforts of varying percentage. We started at 50% of maximum effort for 100m and worked our way up to 100%. However, most of the guys were clearly deaf, as they were running at 100% from the first effort onwards, racing each other for the 100m. The only people running at the correct percentage of effort were me, a couple of other guys and all the girls. I couldn't remember the last time I'd seen such an ego driven display of machismo (probably the last time anyone had watched me train). I stuck it out for a few weeks, as I really enjoyed the sessions, and with doing no cardio-vascular work at all, it at least kept my hand in. But as the nights grew darker and colder I gave the tri club the flick and set about doing nothing but weights.

So here I was four years later back at the track, but thankfully it was completely different. With triathlon being the fastest growing participation sport in UK, the clubs ranks had swelled. It was still 'girl-heavy' but there were almost thirty people at the track, as opposed to ten when I'd been previously in 2002. All the pretentiousness had gone and it was a much friendlier place to be.

The track sessions, however, were to be short lived, as Amy took over an aerobics class on the same evening. If she ran back from the gym, it gave me ten minutes to get to the track on the outskirts of town from our flat in the city centre. Obviously I couldn't simply rock off, as someone had to look after the little lady. So I ended up sacking the track sessions off, which was a mistake, but it was Amy's job. She didn't have to work, but she wanted to do what she could, so she could still retain some feeling of independence and contribution. Amy did bin that evening class off in the end, one week before Ironman....

Like all addictions, it starts small…

Missing the track session sent me into overdrive and panic. In fact any session I missed through work or any other circumstance did. I'd spend ages pouring over my training schedule, which I'd taped inside the cupboard door in the living room, looking at how to accommodate any missing sessions. What could be sacrificed? Which were the priority sessions? Trying to fit all the training in was a massive problem and not being able to do so would stress me out horrendously. I started resenting anyone and anything that interfered with my training. I was either training, thinking about training or working. Note how there's a distinct lack of anything to do with wife and family? My 'daddy-daughter' days, where it was just me and Lilly-Mae having quality time and giving Amy some time to herself, had gone out of the window. Everyone's life had to dance to the tune of my Ironman training. All Amy ever heard me say was 'I've got a session to do…'

Testing with the Superbikes in Spain was coming up in January 2006. How would I train? What could I do? Should I take my bike? The hotel was in the middle of nowhere, and had no pool, so what was I going to do for swimming? Panic, panic, panic! I may have come a long way with the swimming but it was still by far the thing I was most concerned about. I'd yet to swim 1500m in one go, let alone 3800m. Four days without a swim session! How could I make that up? Time to stand gawping at the training schedule on the door again – a fact not lost on Amy, who always had a comment when she saw me stood there. I was actually thinking that having to go to Spain testing with the lads was something that I *didn't* want to do, as I'd rather stay at home and train. Now I know what you're thinking, and you're right. Problem is, no-one was pointing it out to me (apart from Amy who was constantly telling me I'd bitten off more than I could chew), and the only person who could do anything about it was me. I only did three days out of ten in Spain with Honda. Other work commitments meant I couldn't do the full ten, which suited me as that amount of time without access to a pool would've sent me into a panic attack. I did what I could, which was run. I longed to get back to hit the pool and the turbo – what an idiot. I'd completely lost sight of what was going on – then.....

Lilly-Mae had a temperature, in fact such a temperature we had to go to A&E. We went to A&E because the emergency doctor never rang back - well they did – 2 days later. We finally got to A&E, having taken forever to find somewhere to park. After wading through all the lovely people in tracksuits with one hand shoved down their pants, arguing with girlfriends wearing fake gold earrings the size of small dinner plates, who in turn were waiting for their friend who'd been glassed in a bar fight, we got to the triage nurse. I think the NHS do a massively difficult job under extremely difficult circumstances with very few resources. But they are also crippled by bureaucracy making an already difficult job almost impossible.

As we'd gone straight to A&E we hadn't thought to take any baby food (new parents flapping, etc). We asked for something to give her. They had no baby milk, just water, and no bottles or teats. Then the guy who'd gone to get some milk went home. After waiting for an hour I drove home, got everything we needed and drove back to hospital. Having not being fed for five hours meant that she was as distressed from this as she was from the temperature. We then got admitted to a decrepit ward run by stressed out and surly staff, with Lilly-Mae unable to get any sleep, as she was woken up every five minutes by a door being slammed somewhere on the ward. She also had to have a canular inserted, in case she needed an antibiotic drip. This went down really well with her, but rather than take it out when it became apparent she wouldn't need a drip, through lack of communication/shift changes, etc, they left it in all night. Ultimately she would've recovered faster at home than she did in the government-underfunded Dickensian nightmare that is the NHS.

So what's the point of this story? Well, during the day when I was at the flat, Amy had sent me home whist she stayed at the hospital. I had nothing to do for two hours so I did a bike/run. Oh dear. My little girl is in hospital and whilst Amy is with her and I'm at home I do a brick session? What on earth was I thinking?

Yes, I realised that Ironman training had already consumed me, and my family life was suffering. I was working away all day, coming home late to get straight to bed, to spend the next morning on a one hour swim, followed by one hour bike, by which time it was lunchtime and time to crack on with admin at home all afternoon. Then an early night as I'd have to be up at 6 am to swim, to go away with work for the rest of the day (usually involving a three hour drive each way), then get stuck in the usual M6 rush hour nightmare, so my three hour drive home turned into a five hour journey. Then when I did get home it was two hours on the laptop to do the day's admin (Lilly-Mae would already be in bed, so I wouldn't have seen her), followed by going straight to bed because I'd got 'swim 1A' in the morning which was 2100m of drills and sprints over varying distances. I hadn't even started going away with the Superbikes yet on the European Tour.

Time to get a grip.

Chapter 6

Let's start again.....

I'd had the wakeup call I needed. I was taking this far too seriously, mainly due to shitting myself at the huge task ahead of me, and falling into the Ironman trap of thinking that no matter how much you train, you still feel it isn't enough. I also picked up a cold (which I never do) and after taking a week to get over that, as soon as I started training again I developed Plantar Fasciitis, where the ligament under the heel becomes too tight to run. This meant another week off and treatment from trusty *City Physio* in Manchester. Rather than completely freak out about it, I'd already sat down and got my head straight.

You see, Ironman gets inside your head, well it did mine anyway. I couldn't stop thinking about it and constantly fretting as to whether I was doing enough training. Everything had become either 'pre-ironman' or 'post-ironman'. Instead of looking forward to Lilly-Mae's first birthday, I was thinking '…we drive down to Sherborne for Ironman the day after Lilly's birthday….'. I couldn't believe

I'd been so obsessive, I'd forgotten all the reasons why I was doing Ironman in the first place. Having the time off because of my heel meant spending time with the family, and for a short time Lilly-Mae got her dad back and Amy her husband. When my heel had calmed down after physio and keeping on top of it with stretching, I eased myself back into training. I was just getting back into the flow when the first long trip of the year came up in March – Florida and the 'World Golf Fitness Summit'.

This was a three day conference in Disney World, so I decided to take Amy and the little dude along as well. We were supposed to arrive two days before the conference started and were staying on for a week afterwards to do the whole Disney World thing. It was also the first time flying with Lilly-Mae. Were we going to be the people everyone hates on the plane, with a screaming baby? We packed for the journey and we were clearly going overboard on what we needed. As anyone who is a parent knows, babies do require tonnes of stuff, but being relatively new parents meant we were still being a bit over zealous on the packing!

Once we got everything packed and down to some sort of reasonable weight, we left for the airport. I made use of the chauffeur service. It doesn't cost that much more than the normal long term car park, but someone meets you at the terminal and takes your car for you. When you return they meet you outside, which saves pissing about with car park buses when you've got three suitcases, a wife and a nine month old baby in tow. Fortunately for us, Virgin flies direct to Orlando from Manchester, another billy bonus. As flying is officially the most inconvenient way to travel, we'd got to Manchester Airport four hours before flying, to go through the security bollocks.

So we're at the airport four hours before flying, then it's a nine hour flight. We've got enough supplies for the little lady for that time, plus extra. Amazingly for the UK, things go smoothly and as we're travelling with an infant we get ushered through the check in procedure! Great! It then went all downhill from there. The flight was delayed an hour, then two, then four, then six, then cancelled. Having been at the airport for almost ten hours, it was finally binned. Through a fluke, we managed to collect our luggage, find out which hotel we were staying in and that we were leaving on exactly the same flight, just the next day. I'd seen this happen before, so rather than wait for the coaches to arrive to take us to the hotel which was only ten minutes away, we got a taxi. When we arrived at the hotel we were the first to check in. Two hours later people were still being processed at the airport whilst my family were enjoying room service. The next day Virgin were being very careful to point out that the flight hadn't been 'cancelled' but had in fact been 'delayed'. Whatever gimps. Lilly-Mae was fine on the flight – she's a very good baby and not mardy in any way whatsoever. She took it all in her stride and just chilled out. When we arrived the sun was shining and it was time to relax. The taxi took us to the hotel, we got in the room and crashed.

The next day I dragged myself out of bed, jet lagged to the eyeballs. I'd lost a day to get over the jet lag, thanks to Virgin, and had to make use of strong American coffee at breakfast to get myself going. I was attending the conference with the guys from the physio unit that travels around the European Tour, treating the players' injuries. As this was the 'new me' training wasn't a priority and if I could do something I would – but in no way was I going to beat myself up over it. When I returned from the first day of the conference Lilly-Mae was asleep and had been all afternoon apparently. We didn't think anything of it and just put it down to jet lag. She slept right through to 3am – thirteen hours continuously. When she woke up things started to go wrong, she immediately started dry heaving and was clearly not right.

We were concerned, as she hadn't had anything for thirteen hours and just threw up anything we gave her – she was obviously very ill. I called downstairs to the concierge for a cab to take us to the hospital in Orlando. Amy was beside herself with worry, but I just had to explain to her we were in the US now, so A&E would be empty. As you have to pay for your treatment in the US, A&E isn't awash with idiots being treated for all the usual alcohol related problems A&E's in the UK have to deal with. We arrived at the hospital and despite being a Saturday night it was empty (imagine going to Manchester Royal Infirmary A&E on a Saturday night at 4am).

We were seen straight away with two doctors attending to Lilly-Mae. The upshot was she had an ear infection which had caused another temperature. Lilly-Mae had been fiddling with her left ear the week before leaving, so as a precaution we had taken her to the doctors to get it checked out - we didn't want anything drastic happening whilst away, like an ear infection. She was given the all clear. Now here we are in hospital being told she has exactly what we went to the doc's about, in the ear she'd been fussing with. This wrote off the second day of the conference as we didn't get out of the hospital until 10 am. We got back to the hotel and I texted the other guys, letting them know what had happened. But it wasn't all bad - if you're going to be ill, it might as well be in Orlando, with blue skies and sunshine. The conference came to an end and Lilly-Mae was perking up just in time for the Disney World part of the trip.

We basically spent the next week touring the massive parks that comprise Disney World and eating as much crap as possible. In the ten day trip I managed one six mile run! I didn't care though, as it was great time with the family. We did everything available over there, including Cape Canaveral – it was great. We flew back to Manchester and arrived back tanned but horrendously jet lagged – this was a problem as both Amy and myself had the Wilmslow half marathon the day after getting back. Ooops.

The night before the half marathon Amy was trying to talk us both out of doing it. My mum was 'booked' to come down at 8am and assume control of the little dude. I was soooooo tempted to sack the 13 mile run off - you know what jet lag is like – but I'd entered us both into this race before I knew we were going to Orlando. I sold it to Amy on the premise it would 'undo' all the crap we'd eaten over the last ten days and get us back on track. It was 12 midnight and I was still wide awake. I measured my delta and it was 30! Your delta is a basic HR test you can do to see if you're overtrained, etc. You lie still and after two minutes see what your HR is. Mine was 65bpm (10bpm higher than it should be anyway). You then stand up quickly and at the end of two minutes standing see what your HR is again. Mine was 95! The difference between the first HR number and second is your 'delta'. The idea is for it to be as near to zero as possible. Anything under 10 is good, but anything around the 30 mark is a *stay at home and sleep* situation, not *run thirteen miles*. We dragged ourselves out of bed the next morning, with just ten hours sleep in the past forty eight. This could be a nightmare. It was.

We drove to Wilmslow, parked up and made our way to the start. We got into position at the start and with the klaxon we began the 13.2 mile run. And……it wasn't that bad. We took it steady and managed to cover the first half in forty five minutes. At this pace it was going to be a 1hr 30min half marathon – a very respectable time, considering the 'prep' we'd done, and over four minutes faster than my previous time. Unfortunately the jet lag, lack of sleep and general, horrendous fatigue began to set in. My HR began to drop, as did my pace. I was really struggling. Then around the ten mile mark my left knee began to ache badly. I knew exactly what it was. My ITB (ilio-tibial band) had tightened up so badly it was pulling on the outside of my knee. It got so bad I almost had to stop, I eventually dragged my sorry arse across the line in 1hr 49mins - pathetic. I'd slowed to almost 10 minute mile pace towards the end. I felt like I was running through treacle backwards and despite the ITB issue probably couldn't have gone faster anyway.

This was a disaster psychologically, I was much much fitter than the last time I'd run a half marathon and here I was fifteen minutes slower. I had to put this behind me and crack on with training, my cavalier attitude towards training was all well and good, but it hadn't done me any good physically. Suddenly Ironman looked like something I may actually not complete - I had to run twice that distance after cycling 112 miles and swimming 2.4 miles – shit.

After that disaster came the start of the Superbike season and Golf season. Also with that came a tonne more work and the travelling that goes with it – this was going to push my easy going attitude and 'don't get obsessed' outlook on training to the limit. If I was away with the superbikes I either had to take my bike and turbo with me or make do with whatever facilities were on site. I did 180 lengths in a 17m pool on two occasions – character building to say the least. It was the same for the golf, although taking my bike with me was not an option as it involved flying. It all involved getting up at stupid o'clock in the morning or training late at the end of the working day. I never did any of the scheduled sessions I was supposed to, it was a constant battle of compromises whilst trying desperately not to let it get under my skin.

All the time Ironman loomed large in the back of my mind, laughing at me, telling me I wasn't doing enough training, it was all going to end in tears, I was going to fail, *everyone* knew I was doing Ironman and therefore *everyone* was going to know I'd cocked it up. This constant 'making do' simply was what it was – it's what everyone has to put up with. All you can do is make best with what you have and crack on.

Chapter 7

It's all about the bike....

As the weather was getting slightly better I'd decided to venture out on my bike. This was the first time since that pathetic effort at the end of the previous year. I still didn't have any cycling gear and continued to insist on using running gear whilst on the turbo. After another horrendous journey I knew I had to get some cycling kit. A trip to the local bike shop in Manchester and £100 lighter, I came away with the full Lance Armstrong Discovery Channel rig and luminous yellow winter jacket, to at least help car drivers see me. I'd bought some lovely carbon Oakley glasses to wear on the bike, complete with spare yellow lenses, whilst in Orlando, for half the price they were in the bike shop in town – gotta love that VAT! With my new rig came a new enthusiasm to get out on the bike, as opposed to living on the turbo. This is especially important because I didn't know how to 'ride' a bike. That might sound crazy, but instinctive gear changing to maintain cadence and position on the bike are all vital for triathlon. I hadn't learnt any of it, because I'd been on the turbo as opposed to actually going out on my bike.

I realised I had to learn as much about bikes as possible. My only other two wheel experience was owning a string of Suzuki GSX-R's, the latest of which had just been sold to the garage I originally bought it from, as I'd managed to cover a whopping 1500 miles in two years. Most of those 1500 miles were spent on the track, a very expensive habit. Riding hard on the track gave me an understanding of what the Superbike riders were going through, and I knew the tracks they raced on. But it was almost impossible to get out on track now as any spare time was spent training – so the GSX-R had to go.

In an effort to understand more about triathlon I took out a subscription to *'220'* magazine and scoured the internet to learn as much as possible. I normally avoided all magazines training related, as they tend to be full of the same stuff regurgitated. What I mean by that is, there's only so many ways of talking about the same subjects. But surprisingly *'220'* was really helpful, and coach Kiddle was one of the contributors. So rather than run the risk of missing something, I paid up to receive it every month. If you're an amateur triathlete and want to learn as much about the sport as possible in a short space of time then get *'220'*, it will soon bring you up to speed.

The problem with all this research was that I began to learn about things such as *'Dura-Ace'*, *'Ultegra'*, *'full carbon'*. Ignorance was replaced with a small amount of knowledge and I now looked at Renny with its componentry - it all began to look very 'budget'. I could feel the 'fear' coming on – should I upgrade? This was supposed to be cheap, but I did need to give myself the best possible chance, right?

No, no, no, no! I'd told Amy this wasn't going to be a spend-fest. I put all thoughts of spending money on Renny behind me. Amy would have a fit and I hadn't even done a triathlon yet, let alone the IM. I looked at the positives. The LeMonde Reno had decent carbon forks and seat post, but was sporting entry level Shimano Tiagra componentry, apart from the '105' rear mech (ah, the lingo was coming thick and fast now...). The wheels weighed two tonnes but were bullet proof training wheels, ideal for shite UK roads. Being a pure road bike it had a nice geometry that wasn't crippling like a pure time trial bike – it was totally OK. I did sneak the thought of buying some race wheels, and a call to Kiddle while he was having his commode emptied, confirmed that this was the most cost effective way of saving weight.

The time came for a proper ride out, a three hour job. I'd missed all the two hour rides in my schedule up until that point, so this was going to be the first long one. I was also going to attempt it on just water to see exactly what would happen. I already knew what the answer was, I was going to struggle mightily for energy and would experience this drop off severely, as well as struggling to keep my HR up. I was doing this for two reasons, Firstly I needed to *feel* exactly what this was like, so I could recognise it, should something like it happen during Ironman. I'm not talking about *hitting the wall* - total glycogen depletion - just a severe drop off in energy levels as you approach *the wall*. Secondly my body only knew how to use carbohydrate for energy, it had no clue how to use fat. So I had to start forcing my body to use fat as an energy source - something it wasn't very good at. I set off, concentrating on cadence and sticking to my HR limits. Constantly stopping at traffic lights on my way out of the city centre was infuriating, but something I would learn to live with. After 45 minutes I'd made it to Alderly Edge in one piece, despite the gauntlet of the A34.

Then a funny feeling - I looked down and had a flat rear tyre. I had to learn to change a tyre at some point, and rather now than on Ironman. It took ten long minutes, as I hadn't changed a puncture since riding a BMX, but it was all done relatively painlessly and I was off again. I really enjoyed it, it was great to be out in the country. I watched the miles roll on the trip computer (another unforeseen purchase from the bike shop at £25, as I had to have the cordless one obviously) and the time. When it got to 1½ hours I simply turned around and headed back. I covered fifty miles in those three hours, which was OK for a first 'long' ride, although I felt terrible. Surviving on just water meant I was totally on empty when I got back, something I knew would happen, but as I said it was something I had to *feel*. I also put this down as a contributing factor to me falling off the bike at a set of traffic lights, feet still clipped into the pedals! Something else I was still getting used to - unclipping before stopping. At least it gave the people at the lights a giggle. Everything worked fine on Renny as well. I had to make a slight adjustment to the handlebars but that was it. The bike had been measured for me using bike fitting software at SBR sports. Getting this measurement right becomes more important the longer the distance, and 112 miles is a long way. Bike position is something you tend to fiddle with over time, hence time spent on the bike is never wasted.

Next time out on the bike, and another puncture! Again I repaired it and rocked off trying to cover more distance in the same time. My rides were working out to one long ride per week at this stage, and would stay that way until Ironman. A long ride at this stage was three hours (these would increase to six hours eventually). Short, twenty minute runs were also introduced after these long rides, but runs of up to an hour were de rigueur after the *'short'* rides and would go up to two hours eventually. I got another puncture the next ride out. This was ridiculous, I don't mind changing a puncture, but having to stop every time out is a little too much. Another trip to the bike shop and some Bontrager puncture resistant tyres were whacked on – they had a higher rolling resistance but that was a good thing as far as I was concerned, it all added to the training. The problem was the rear where I'd been getting all the punctures, the turbo had been taking a tiny layer of rubber off every time I used it, and over the months this meant the rear was paper thin, making a puncture inevitable. After fitting the new tyres, punctures were a thing of the past!

I picked a route and worked out an 18 mile 'loop' that incorporated some decent hills. I became intimately familiar with this loop, the change in road surface and its effect on speed, manhole covers, potholes, hidden entrances, etc. The riding position became more and more important, and another trip to the bike shop saw the purchase of some Profile Design 'Ironman' branded carbon tri bars (£100). Again I felt a bit of a geek buying Ironman branded stuff, having not actually done an Ironman, but these were the 'official' tri bars of Ironman, therefore a 'must buy' in my eyes. The Discovery Channel kit was taking a real hammering, so hot on the heels of the tri bars I went to 'Decathlon' to get some more cycling kit and a bike bag – another £120! Having sold the idea of triathlon to Amy on the premise it wasn't that expensive the £'s were racking up!

With the tri bars came something else to fiddle with in terms of position. How close together to have them, how long or short to have them, pointing slightly up, down, level with ground. The first time I tried them I nearly crashed. Unused to steering the bike with them, I was too ham-fisted with the input and nearly creamed in. For some reason, cycling became something I really looked forward to. After every session I'd go through the trip computer to see what my average speed was, always looking for 18½ mph. I knew that was a good average speed, especially considering a third of the ride was through the traffic light and roundabout fest that is Kingsway in Manchester. Cycling through the Cheshire countryside was so peaceful and calming, even though I was working hard on the bike. Once I was in the sticks, away from everyone trying to run me over on the urban roads, I could really get into a groove mentally. Being on the bike meant time alone with my own thoughts, again something I was going to do a lot of during an Ironman. You need to be really comfortable with your own head, so the long rides were invaluable for that reason alone.

May was fast approaching and the first race of the year. Everything seemed to be coming together, even the swimming, and I was looking forward to breaking my triathlon duck. I wasn't nervous about Eton, I was so focused on Ironman that Eton was just a short, sharp training session. I didn't know what to expect, and how hard could it be anyway?

Chapter 8

Eton Super Sprints, super slow.......

May arrived and with it my first race and first ever triathlon in the form of Eton Super Sprints. Now I had to start thinking about the intricacies of multi-sport, including the transitions. Up until that point I'd viewed transitions as something not to be rushed - rushing would surely mean mistakes, so you might as well take your time – and that had been my original plan. I ran this past Kiddle who nearly choked on the phone (probably a Werther's Original). He explained that transitions were something to be smashed through toute suite, and they can make a massive difference to your overall time - the shorter the tri, the more important the transition. Kiddle had done a great piece in *'220'* about transitions and the importance of them. I looked through the article in *'220'* and sure enough it was gold dust. There were so many things I hadn't even thought about - I won't bore you with the details as this isn't a training book – but I will say a good transition *could* make your race, but a bad one will *definitely* ruin it.

We'd booked into a B&B in Windsor and travelled down on the Friday ready for the race on Sunday. Lilly-Mae was running my mum ragged for the weekend, so I could prep uninterrupted. I packed my kit and double checked everything, using the list from '*220*'. Obviously there was tonnes of stuff I was missing - elastic laces, anti-fog drops, elastic bands, spare laces, clear goggles (I was actually going to do the swim in my tiny ultra dark speedo goggles!). I made a list of what I was missing with a view to buying it from SBR on the Saturday. The list was endless and involved yet more expense, a fact not lost on Amy.

We arrived at the B&B after a tedious 5 hour drive and peeled ourselves out of the car. The B&B was a real 'homely' place and we settled into our room for a power nap. I had the day off training so I was fresh for the race the next day, but unlike everyone else racing (unless they were doing Ironman) I had a 45 minute cool down run to do as soon as I finished the race. This extra run was all part of IM training and the plan was to treat this race as a threshold training session with transition experience. Sounds very nonchalant, 'treat it as a training session', but that's how I was looking at it - I had no reason to think of it in any other way.

The day before the race was glorious, sunny and warm. We went to SBR to collect all the bits and pieces I needed from my list but everyone else had obviously had the same idea, as they had sold out of most things apart from the goggles. I bought the standard Aqua-Sphere Eagles, which most people wear as they're comfy, and more importantly, you can see where you're going. It was only after Kiddle pointed out that I wasn't about to swim in a lit swimming pool where you can see the bottom with a handy line down the middle, so you know which direction you're going in, that I realised how important these were.

We headed back to the B&B and it was at this point I realised I hadn't actually worn my wetsuit since trying it on five months earlier! Doh! Time for some impromptu wetsuit training in the shower back at the B&B – Amy was in hysterics! If I could get out of it in five seconds or less that was good enough. I poured myself into the wetsuit and soaked myself in the shower, jumping out and following Kiddle's instructions. I was able to get out in less than five seconds – great! I also put the new goggles on for three seconds to adjust them. As far as I was concerned, that was them ready to go. Idiot.

After a fitful night's sleep we got up and had breakfast – I wasn't as nervous as I thought I would be, just slightly anxious which was more excitement than anything else. I wasn't concerned with the distances involved, but I was about to race with other 'triathletes' and any shortcomings would be there for everyone to see. We packed up and headed down to Dorney Lake where the tri was being held, parked up and made the 1000m walk from the car park to the registration tent, which gave me plenty of opportunity to check the other competitors out. Serious looking triathletes with carbon bikes were everywhere, all looking like they'd done this a million times before,. But had they? I convinced myself they 'had all the gear but no idea', to ease the nerves and the bike envy.

I also noticed the other aspect of triathlon race day – what t-shirt to wear. Everyone was wearing some sort of t-shirt from another triathlon or some such event. Personally I've never seen the point of wearing a t-shirt from a previous year's event – all you're doing is advertising the fact that you're wearing at least a year old t-shirt and are a tight bugger! Clearly this was some sort of triathlon etiquette I was unaware of. Maybe I should've dig my *'BUPA Great Run'* t-shirt out or something similar, but a 10km run t-shirt surely wasn't good enough to wear at a triathlon?

I'd done an event called *'Tough Guy'* a number of times in previous years and was even in the winning team once in 1996. For those of you that don't know, *Tough Guy* isn't the name of gay night at a Manchester night club, but a ridiculous event around a horse sanctuary near Wolverhampton. It consists of a horrendous cross country run followed by an outrageous two mile long assault course, which you have to do twice. You spend 99% of your time either up to your knees in mud, in water, or crawling, or all three. Maybe I should've worn one of my Tough Guy tops? Then again who wants to walk around with a top on that says *'Tough-Guy'*? I may as well grow a moustache and start wearing butt-less leather chaps.

I made my way to registration, got my helmet checked and picked up my race number. I had my bike racked with plenty of time to relax – except I couldn't. I must have checked my kit a hundred times, I was sure I was missing something and was surprised at the level of nerves I was experiencing. It was cold and a stiff wind was blowing across the rowing lake, the good weather forecast was no-where to be seen and it was the total opposite to the sunny, clear day before. Amy and I had time to watch the start of the waves before mine. It was a 'deep water' start, meaning everyone was already in the water. A horn sounded and the relatively peaceful lake was turned into a white water melee. After around 100m there were at least three people clinging to each of the three rescue canoes. Why was that? Hadn't they trained for this triathlon? I was about to find out.

With 20 minutes to go and after thirty visits to the toilet (including an unfortunate episode of anal devastation in the club house - sorry to whoever went in after me) I put my wetsuit on and headed to the swim start with the rest of my age group wave. Everyone started to jump in and I followed suit. I then came rocketing back out of the water like a trident missile launched from a nuclear submarine. I had absolutely no open water swimming experience whatsoever – I didn't think it was important - and how hard could it be anyway? Surely having to stop and turn every 25m in a pool was more of an arse than being able to swim free for the whole distance in a drag saving wetsuit? What an idiot. Once I'd stopped hyperventilating, I tried to listen to the swim brief in the middle of the swim pack, when all of a sudden the start klaxon sounded.

All the stories of the swim start I'd heard were true, and from here on the swim start shall be known as 'aqua-ruck'. It was like a bar fight, apart from you weren't in a bar, it wasn't preceded with drink and merriment, you were wearing a wetsuit and had to swim in a lake. I was punched, kicked, my right goggle immediately filled up with water as it didn't fit properly, and my wetsuit was also trying to strangle me. I nearly panicked and after 100m was having serious doubts about finishing the swim. Jesus! 400m should take me no more than 7½ mins and here I was going so slowly that the wind was blowing me along! All thoughts of not finishing had to be put aside, not because I was a double tough storm trooper but because the cold water was beginning to grip my arms and legs, meaning I had to thrash them to keep them going.

A quick look around and I could see the rescue canoes were busy with several people clinging onto them. I could only manage breaststroke. After five months of training and getting myself to a reasonable standard where I felt confident I could do at least 1500m, here I was in front of everyone, including Amy, breast-stroking like a tit. I'd put my wetsuit on incorrectly, I hadn't squeezed my shoulder blades together when the zip was done up and Amy had done the Velcro so tight it would take a three mile high tidal wave travelling at 400mph to undo it.

I eventually got to the end of the swim and was helped out of the water with plenty of spectators watching. I felt a complete idiot in my 'Ironman' wetsuit. Yeah, nice one, geek - a piece of litter could've floated round quicker than I did. I sprinted through transition taking my wetsuit off as I ran, trying to regain some element of respectability and pride. Helmet on and I ran through transition bare foot with my bike, just to run all the way back again to get my race number. I ran back out of transition and jumped onto my bike as I went, my shoes were already clipped in but held upright by elastic bands. Having them clipped in but bouncing off the floor as you run through transition runs the risk of them popping off the pedal, apparently. I did consider simply putting my cycling shoes on and running through transition, which Kiddle strongly advised against. Watching two people go flying on the concrete, wearing their shoes, confirmed he was right. A quick look down at the old HRM showed 11mins on the clock. What a disaster.

On the bike and it was time to get a move on. My woefully slow swim meant I was at least fresh for the bike and I began to hammer it. It was a four lap affair around the lake and was a closed road, which meant no myopic car drivers to worry about. This type of 'lap' arrangement suits me as I can attack each lap as a one off. Here the varied nature of multisport at this level, and its competitors, really showed itself and why it's a great sport to take part in. Whilst being overtaken by an 'elite' on a trick carbon bike, I was simultaneously overtaking a bloke on a mountain bike complete with mirrors, tassels on the handlebars and baby seat on the back. I half expected him to give me a tinkle on his bell as I passed.

The biting wind wasn't biting anymore after the cold of the lake but was more or less directly in your face on the 'out' leg of the bike. This didn't bother me too much and rather than try to make time in a head wind I simply tried to maintain pace, using the return leg to go for it with the wind behind me. I tried to keep up with every fast guy that passed me for as long as possible, dragging me along without drafting them whilst chasing down any slow rider in front of me. There were all sorts of bits by the side of the road - water bottles, tool kits, a single tri bar, a cycling shoe. How had that happened? I passed at least three people pushing bikes back to transition with flat tyres. Imagine travelling all that way just to get a flat? What a bastard.

After two laps I caught and passed a huge gaggle of riders from my wave - I was making good time. The bike flashed by and I blasted towards the dismount area. I'd already slipped my feet out of my shoes (another *220*/Kiddle tip which may seem obvious) unlike the guy in front, who came to a complete stop, still clipped in, and keeled over. Running through transition trying to find my spot was a nightmare. My selection of a white towel was perhaps not the most inspired choice in amongst all the other towels, which were white. I eventually found my spot and chucked my bike onto the rack, put my trainers on and sprinted through transition to the run start. As I crossed the run start, a quick glance at the HRM showed 39mins on the clock.

Was this good or bad? Did it matter, after floating round the swim like a single cell amoeba? I had no idea.

The run was a two lap job, up and back in a straight line parallel to the lake. This could've been demoralising but with plenty of people to overtake, I didn't have time to think about it. The good thing about this sport is that you can have a crap swim, like me, then maybe make it up on the bike and run. I felt surprisingly 'ok' on the run, which immediately placed a seed of self doubt in my mind as to whether I'd gone hard enough on the bike. I felt like I could maybe go that bit faster but was paranoid about running out of steam – my lack of experience really showed itself. I had my HRM obviously and religiously kept my HR around the 160bpm mark, but over sprint distance could I afford to be a bit more cavalier and go for 170bpm? Or would that be the end of my race? As the last km approached I upped the pace slightly, keen to get a sub 22 minute 5km, sneaking into the 170bpm HR zone. As the line approached a huge sense of relief stole over me, I crossed the line in 1 hour 13 minutes.

I went through transition and met Amy, as a steady stream of people finished. A quick race debrief with her consisted mainly of the horrendous swim, and had she seen me practically stationary at the back of the pack? The sense of relief that I'd experienced just before I crossed the line soon started to disappear as I began to break the race down into its parts. I made my way to my rack position to towel dry and get a dry t-shirt on for the 45 minute cool down run. Transition was still busy as the age group waves were still going, I wondered if any of them had cocked the swim up, like me? After sorting myself out and getting a dry top on, I picked Amy up at the transition entrance to start the 45 minute run. As we jogged out of Dorney Lake we watched the steady stream of people who were still on the bike and run, as the age group waves continued. The people that were leaving looked on as if I was crazy, but the 45 minute run went some way to relieving the disappointment of the race. After running out for 22½ minutes we simply turned round and headed back to the lake to collect my things and head home.

As I wheeled my bike out of transition the last of the waves were out on the run and transition was nothing but empty racks, with a few bikes dotted about the place. Wearing my *'Eton Super Sprints'* top, we headed to the car and the long drive back to Manchester. I could already feel the 'fear' coming on.

Chapter 9

Eton, the aftermath

I was pleased to get my first triathlon out of the way and gain some valuable race experience. But the post race demons set in as soon as we got back to Manchester. I went online and began to pour over the race results, going through all the *'what if'* scenarios. This is classic triathlete behaviour, going through results and obsessively looking where you can save time. My transitions were fine (apart from forgetting to put my number belt on for the bike and having to go back for it), but the *'what if'* scenario applied mainly to the swim. The swim had been a disaster I hadn't seen coming. I had no idea that open water swimming was so different and my confidence had shattered. How was I supposed to swim like that for 2.4 miles? Was I going to breaststroke the whole thing?! First Wilmslow and now Eton. My season couldn't have got off to a worse start psychologically.

I'd also been too conservative on the bike. I could have gone at least two minutes quicker, which is a lot in a sprint triathlon. Had I swam the 400m as I should've been able, combined with the bike, I could've got my time down to the 1hr 5 min mark. I was racked with disappointment, although outwardly I said all the right things about gaining experience, learning, etc. Inside though, I was gutted and slightly embarrassed.

I'd been training for five months and the end result was a disaster as far as I was concerned, and an expensive one so far. The trip to Eton had cost over £200 with accommodation, fuel, food, etc. I'd lost nearly 6kg in weight by now and my weight training sessions had been completely sacrificed, my arms and arse had disappeared. I thought I'd got the swimming under control – Kiddle said he'd like to have me down to a sub 33 minute 1500m in the 25m pool by this stage and I'd actually got it down to 28 minutes – I felt like I was ahead of the game. Another target of his was a 30 minute 10 mile time trial time on the bike, which again I could do easily. So to go to Eton and completely mess it up was hard to take. I obviously wasn't as far ahead of the game as I thought. Self doubt started to creep in big time.

All the sessions I'd missed through work or whatever reason over the last five months came back to haunt me. Had I been too cavalier in trying not to become 'obsessed'? Taking it all in my stride was all well and good, but was the reality of Ironman training that you *had* to be obsessed? With my confidence broken the task of getting myself from triathlon virgin to Ironman began to sink in – had I taken on too much? Amy kept telling me I shouldn't have jumped feet first into a full Ironman and that I should've stuck to my original 18 month plan of completing a half Ironman before tackling the full one. I began to come to the conclusion that maybe she was right.

Whilst nine months was maybe plenty of time to train for a full Ironman, with a full time job plus wife and baby daughter, maybe it wasn't? A confidence call was placed to Kiddle, he was instructed to send me new schedules that were prioritised – sessions in red were *'must do'*, green for *'should do'* and black for *'could do'*. I had to get a grip on the training and make sure I was maximising the time I had available. This meant my week now looked something like this:

Monday
Recovery Run 25 mins – black
Bike 2 hours inc 6x90 secs of threshold – both green
Swim 3A – 3200m of various sprints etc

Tuesday
Run 1hr 30mins – both green
Swim 1 – 1000m

Wednesday
Swim 10 - 800m – green
Bike 1hr – both black
Run 1hr

Thursday
Stretch 10 mins - black

Friday
Bike 50 mins easy spin – both black
Swim 1A – 2100m

Saturday
Run 2hrs – both red sessions
Bike 2hrs

Sunday
Swim 9 – 45mins at race pace - black
Bike 3hrs 30mins – both red
Run 40mins

With this new system I could prioritise my sessions and see instantly which ones I had to do – as long as I did all the red sessions and as many of the green as possible, Kiddle told me I should be OK. I hoped so. I had to put Eton behind me, learn from it and crack on. I'd entered Ironman and that was it. Just as I said at the beginning of this book, doing an Ironman is like doing a parachute jump – you're going to hit the ground, it's just a question of how hard.

I was getting into the 2-3 hour runs by this time, all at marathon pace, which is nice and steady, but still a long time to be running. Obviously the marathon was going to take me anywhere from 4 hours to 5½ hours come Ironman day, depending on how things went, so I couldn't complain too much about these runs. But where do you run for that amount time when you live in Manchester city centre? As with the bike rides, I had to negotiate my way past hundreds of sets of traffic lights, and running through city centres isn't exactly inspiring, not to mention chowing down on diesel fumes from buses. It may have seemed straight forward to Kiddle from his old people's home in the country, with cross country run routes and scenic rides on his doorstep. All I had on my doorstep was city streets full of litter and rent boys

There is a tow path that runs past our flat. It isn't ideal but it was at least off the main roads. So when a two or three hour run was on the cards I used to run down the path for an hour, turn round and run back, etc, until I'd done 3 hours. It wasn't ideal, but what is when you're training for an Ironman? Unless you can take nine months off and relocate to California to train solely for it.

Another reason for running down the tow path was familiarity with the route. I had my HRM and the zones I needed to work in for a given session, but by using the same route all the time, I could gauge my progress when repeating sessions and use 'feel' as well as my HRM. I preferred this method of measuring my fitness rather than fitness testing. I'm not a huge fan of fitness testing as it doesn't give you the whole picture. All a fitness test does is tell you what's happening at that time on that day – so they can be misleading as far as I'm concerned. At the beginning of this training programme I had some rudimentary testing with Kiddle, which is necessary to provide a starting point. But I don't believe you should measure progress solely by testing. If you do a fitness test, you may have an absolute blinder and set your *actual* PB for whatever you're doing. However, when you come to do the same thing again weeks later, you may have, unbeknownst to you, a 'bad day' and show only a marginal improvement over the last test. This could not only be a huge psychological blow, as you don't think you're improving as much as you should, but could lead you to make unnecessary adjustments to your programme to correct a perceived lack of progress. So by using the same routes all the time I could see week by week if I was improving in terms of economy and RPE (rate of perceived exertion) and adjust my training accordingly from that. Obviously I had my HRM but, ever the squaddie at heart, my reaction to relying on my HRM was - what if it stops working mid session or mid race?

I was able to use a combination of *'feel'* and my HRM so that should my HRM pack in during a session or race, I could at least work at what *'felt'* like the right intensity. I didn't want to rely solely on my Polar HRM which was temperamental. The tow path run took me under several railway bridges with high voltage power lines. My HRM really didn't like that and would register an HR of 270bpm or something similarly ridiculous, until it eventually calmed down after some minutes. I'd have *'markers'* on the run route which I knew I was supposed to be at for certain sessions in a certain time for a given HR. If I was inching in front of them every session I knew I was improving. I could also check the degradation of my performance during the whole run. If I was doing a 60 minute session then I simply ran out for 30 minutes, then turned around and ran back. I'd see if I made it back to my start point, or fall short of it, and if so by how much. The permutations you can use in a single session whether it's a run or bike, to check you're progress, are endless, and as far as I'm concerned ten times more valuable than waiting 6 weeks at a time to see how you perform in a one off test, or a series of tests in a day.

Anyway, back to the tow path and a major downside to running down it - the psychotic Canadian Geese. The nearer the city centre the more chilled out they are as they're used to people, but the further down the tow path you get the more violent they get. I didn't realise this until one hour into a two hour run down the path, when I came across a few geese stood right in the middle of the path. Thinking nothing of it I simply carried on running towards them as I normally did, except this time it kicked right off. The geese went mental and I found myself re-enacting Alfred Hitchcock's *'The Birds'*, with the crows being replaced by huge geese. I got away with only scratches and bruises. Those geese were very handy - when I got home Amy looked at me and asked what had happened, I told her about being dusted up by the geese, and yet again she was in hysterics at me. However, when we went running down the tow path together a few days later, some of the handy ones were in the way. She wasn't laughing then!

Crazy geese aside, I had to start thinking about Lilly-Mae's first birthday – where we were going to have it? When exactly? Her actual birthday was just five days before Ironman - at least I could knock myself out on birthday cake! It was tough to try and think about birthday celebrations, as my mind was full of Ironman and the very real doubt as to whether I was going to complete it – trying to put Eton behind me didn't seem to be working.

I struggled on with the training, juggling work and home life. Just in case I wasn't busy enough, the opportunity came up to become nutritionist to Reading FC. I'd been down to see them the previous season as the conditioner is a mate. I sat down with him and the physio to go through a broad strategy. They both liked what I had to say, but being halfway through the season it was a bit late to start changing things. Winning promotion to the Premiership meant moving things up a gear, including getting a nutritionist on board. Long story short, I talked myself into the job, which I was proud of myself for doing. I don't have a degree in dietetics, or any other degree for that matter - whilst my peers were at university, I was patrolling the streets of Northern Ireland and Bosnia. I do have a diploma in nutrition, which is fine and is the same qualification as the RFU's nutritionist, so I'm not completely incompetent.

But not having a sports science degree in my line of work meant I was at an academic disadvantage and had to work hard to justify my position. Even so, I was doing OK and had got great results from all the athletes and teams I'd worked with. It's not just about having qualifications coming out of your arse, it's about being able to practically apply that knowledge and connect with the athlete. If they don't buy into you or what you're saying, you'll get nowhere with them. This is where my northern monkey-ness came in, and being an ex-squaddie meant that in the banter-filled world of elite sport, I could hold my own. This new job meant a trip down to Reading once a week, beginning in pre-season July with a 4am start to make the drive down. Despite being a great opportunity, all I could think about was that this was something else to completely cock my training schedule up. You've got to love that Ironman training and what it does to you mentally!

I ploughed through May and headed for June, which had my first Olympic distance race in it. Once again due to work I missed all the open water swim sessions at Salford Quays, which played on my mind massively. I had to swim 1500m in the Thames at Windsor. I could do that in 28 minutes in a 25m pool, which should equate to 25 or 26 minute 1500m time in open water, with a wetsuit on. I was desperate to put the demons of Eton to bed and smash a good swim time out.

I'd just have to crack the Red Bull out and power past everyone fuelled on caffeine! I'd been using the Red Bull not just for the obvious reasons (i.e. I had a limitless free supply) but because it was a great training aid. Yes, caffeine does what it does and we all know what its uses are in training, but besides the physiological effects I used it for the psychological benefits. If I had a can of Red Bull then I 'had' to go training, and when you've got a 3 hour run in front of you or whatever, you need all the help you can get.

Chapter 10

Windsor Olympic Triathlon

June arrived and with it fantastic weather. It was a spectacular heat wave, with all the tabloids running pictures of packed British beaches on the front page and headlines of *'phwooar blimey! ran out of ice cream'*, etc. Training in this weather and cycling in particular was much easier. It made you want to go out, as opposed to looking at the grey skies, despondently wondering where global warming was, and the climate of southern France that was supposed to go with it. Granted, global warming would mean that East Anglia would be submerged under the North Sea, but was that a bad thing?

Team Roberts arrived in Windsor the day before the race to register and rack my bike. Lilly-Mae was once more with my mum, as waking her up for the 5am start race day would've meant a world of pain for everyone. Royal Windsor is a big triathlon and it appears to take over the whole town, it seems like every other person is there to take part or is with someone who is. Registering was the usual rigmarole of sizing everyone up, checking out the various event t-shirts people were wearing and trying to gauge their ability from that. I found myself imagining people having bogus event t-shirts made up to deliberately psyche people out at registration. What would they say? *'I ran up Everest using only one lung'*, *'I did Ironman carrying a small pony'*. All I had was my 'Eton Super Sprints' top which had been consigned to Amy's stock of 'comfies' to wear around the house. Besides, my Eton top actually said 'swam like a complete gimp' as far as I was concerned.

Another thing you encounter at registration is the nervous banter. Everyone is slightly fractious and that's natural, but the over friendly, speaking-slightly-too-loudly banter can make you look like a fool – which is why I kept my mouth shut, as I would no doubt say something that would cause a complete 'tumbleweed' moment in the tent. Besides, I was doing a good job of making myself look like an idiot already, with my mouth shut.

I racked my bike and taped two Power Bar gels to my top tube. Another gel would be laid next to my trainers in the morning when I arrived. The bike is where you get the food on board, and by now I was using Power Bar products as opposed to the SiS I'd been using. Power Bar is the official supplement of Ironman and what would be available at the event – so best to start training with it and get used to it. As we left the transition area, Amy pointed out all the people who'd left their water bottles already on their bikes full of their chosen energy drink. It was the middle of a heat wave with temperatures soaring above 30° – we both joked about the boiled drink they'd be enjoying during the race the next day. I on the other hand, in a rare display of forward thinking, was going to put my water bottles in the fridge at the B&B for the night, topped up with ice cubes in the morning, another top tip from '220'.

We spent the rest of the day enjoying the sunshine and walking around Windsor, eating ice cream. The great weather and party atmosphere gave me a good vibe for race day. My wave start was 7.35am which meant a very early breakfast, but I was looking forward to my first OD race. I bought all the spare bits I needed from the triathlon expo (the £'s kept racking up...) - SBR didn't have anything that I needed in stock when I'd called in the previous week on my way home from Reading, as they were struggling to keep up with demand. Triathlon is the fastest growing sport in UK! We topped the day off with some excellent fish and chips to provide that all important race fuel for the next day, before heading back to the B&B to try and get some sleep. I also had my usual extra run to do after the race - an hour cool down run which Amy would do with me. I hoped I'd have a better post race debrief to go through this time.

We had to get up at 5am in time for me to have breakfast and get down to the start. Stumbling around like a myopic mole, I tried desperately to get my race head on. By the time we got down to the transition area at 6am the first race was just starting, I had enough time to make the final prep to my bike, putting the ice cold drinks bottles in the cages. I laid my trainers out with a gel next to them – everything was to hand. It was then time to hurry up and wait for my start.

Sure enough though, the pre-race nerves gripped me and I found myself queuing for the portaloos. These things are never a nice place to be at any time, let alone at 6.30am after spending the previous day baking in the heat. As per

Eton, some rather unfortunate nerve related anal devastation occurred, made doubly devastating by the fact there was no loo roll – PERFECT! Didn't I read in *'220'* somewhere about taking loo roll to transition for this very reason? There was a tiny stamp sized piece of paper which I briefly considered using, but I knew it was pointless. I just had to bite the bullet and pull my pants up, besides I was about to swim 1500m in the Thames which was full of duck shit anyway. I got back to the car walking like John Wayne and informed Amy of the portaloo episode, which she found hilarious.

It was time to squeeze the wetsuit on – and I was *determined* to have a good swim after the Eton Sprint debacle. After putting my wetsuit on, then taking it off as I'd forgotten to put my HRM on - I trotted down to the swim start and eased myself into the Thames for a warm up (with my nice pink swim cap our wave had to wear). I tried to warm up and get used to the water but every time my head went under I went into a hyperventilating fit. Not only that, but once again I hadn't squeezed my shoulder blades together before the wetsuit was zipped up and the velcro was throttling me. After flapping about for a short time, I realised I hadn't given myself enough time to get used to the water and stop this 'gag' reflex I was experiencing every time my head went under the water. This was mistake number 1. Mistake number 2 was to find myself at the front of the start. After the starter's advice not to drink the water - ? - he sounded the horn and the aqua-ruck commenced.

Being at the front meant people were swimming into me, over me and across me. It was the usual chaos and it was everyone for themselves. I felt my foot connect with someone's face. A quick glance at my HR monitor showed 170bpm - not good. Once again my wetsuit was trying to strangle me and I ended up adopting a crawl/breaststroke arrangement, with my HR rocketing. Being in the middle of the river I wasn't sure what to do, but I was rapidly going backwards so I had to do something. I swam to the bank and stood up to undo the velcro on my wetsuit. Someone actually shouted at me not to give up! Jesus, could I balls this up any more than I already had? Now I've got spectators thinking I'm jacking it in.

With that rectified I got back in and swam to the turn buoy in 20 minutes, another open water swim disaster. After turning onto the return leg I managed to get into a rhythm approaching what I'm capable of and made it back to the finish in just over 13 minutes, blasting past lots of people and nearly missing the finish point in my rush. I exited the water and as I ran past Amy, a quick glance at the watch showed 33 minutes – not a total write off, but still 5 minutes slower than what I was capable of.

It was a 100m run into transition and I'd placed a union jack on the floor by my bike so I could find it, after the white towel drama of Eton. I got straight to my bike with the help of the UJ and made a note of how far up the rack it was, using a large tree as a landmark (yet another Kiddle/220 tip). I'd already peeled my wetsuit down to my waist on the 100m run to the bike racks, so all I had to do was step out of it whilst putting my helmet on. As I got to my bike someone was lying on the floor unable to get theirs off, nearly crying. I grabbed Renny and sprinted through transition onto the gravel by the exit in bare feet, where I adopted more of a hopping action like a cat on a hot tin roof! I bombed off onto the 40km single loop bike course and began to overtake people straight away (only the 60+ age group that is) and as per my race plan, every time a 'fast' guy came past I stayed with them as long as possible.

I had to be very careful not to draft though, as this is illegal at amateur level and they have marshals all over keeping an eye out - you'll get a 2 minute penalty, or worse be disqualified. I also kept the fluids up, drinking plenty of my Power Bar energy drink which was still nice and cool.

The miles flashed by, and so did the amount of people fixing punctures. Super slick low rolling resistance tyres are also 'super puncture prone', so the time they would've saved over 25 miles by using them was wiped out ten times over by having to stop and fix a puncture. I got into a groove and found myself in a race with '*Oxford tri bloke*' and '*tall bloke on carbon bike*'. This went on for miles as we kept overtaking each other, but they both eventually succumbed somehow (or more likely had punctures) and I left them with 10 miles to go.

I concentrated on keeping the cadence high and my HR around the 160bpm mark. Best case scenario for me was a 1hr 15 minute bike leg. I'd done ten mile time trials in 30 minutes on open roads, so it wasn't unreasonable to expect to do twenty five miles over an hour and fifteen minutes in a race environment. I loved being in a 'race'. I'd forgotten about the nightmare swim and seemed to be making good time on the bike, for me anyway. I was able to maintain on the hills and push down them, which is the trick - keep powering constantly. Being surrounded by other competitors was so different to the solitary training rides in Manchester, dodging boy racers in Citroen Saxo's, pensioners in Micra's and '*white van man*' with a mobile permanently glued to the ear. I was here in the countryside actually racing and it was a fantastic feeling. Every fifteen minutes I drank a gulp of water or energy drink, and every thirty minutes I downed an energy gel. I was very conscious of dehydrating on the run leg as it was incredibly hot the previous day and would be even hotter during the run, so now was the time to get fluid on board.

Blasting down the country roads I could see an illegal Pelaton up ahead. With no marshals around, a group of ten or so fast riders had formed. We were under strict instructions not to ride two abreast as the roads were not closed, but here was a Tour de France style group with a Mercedes A class stuck behind them. As I approached there was a twitch in the group, forcing one rider onto the wrong side of the road, missing an oncoming Range Rover by millimetres. This near fatal accident seemed to momentarily stun the group, so I took my opportunity! I cut the A class Merc up and stormed through the middle of the group, leaving them is disarray. A brief look behind showed that they had all spread out into single file as they tried to chase me down. Eventually, one by one, they re-took me, but it was great while it lasted. For those few minutes it was like being in my own mini Tour de France, and I didn't feel like the amateur I was.

Back into Windsor, and after nearly taking a fat copper out on traffic duty who was standing in the way as much as possible, I hammered to transition. The roads were lined with spectators cheering you on, the town had been taken over by them – it was a real lift. I came back into transition with race staff frantically waving to slow down. I jumped off my bike and ran into transition. 2nd rack from the fence and near the portaloos was my spot. I ran up the rack and could see my UJ on the floor. I noticed the bikes either side of me were also back, in fact the rack seemed to be extremely full. I convinced myself they were from earlier waves and not my own.

I stuffed my trainers on, boshed another power gel down

and out onto the run. By this time it was 9.30am and it was beginning to get warm – it had been 30° the day before and it was forecast the same for race day. With such an early start I hoped to have the race and the hour long recovery run finished before the sun could begin to melt me. The run was three laps around Windsor town centre with a very cheeky, very steep hill in the middle of it. My legs felt OK and I set off using the same strategy as the bike - stay with fast guys as long as possible and overtake as many as possible. The run route was lined with huge crowds, and the three lap system gave family and friends plenty of opportunity for pictures and encouragement. It also gave you a good opportunity to split time yourself and give advance warning of any impending, heat related disaster. Of the three water stops, one had been added that morning because of the weather, I knew which one it was, as the water tasted like a swimming pool! It had been sterilised using tablets and I recognised the taste from my time in the forces. It didn't bother me, as I'd drunk gallons of sterilised water in the jungles of Belize, but plenty of people were spitting it back out. I knew that jungle training would pay off one day...

During the first lap an Ironman triathlete came past me, well over 6ft and quite muscular. He loped past and off into the distance - he'd probably started a few waves after me. I knew he was an Ironman because he had his IM 'Hawaiian' themed gear on and the 'M-Dot' tattoo – which in this case, he was allowed to wear. I looked on in awe and envy - he made it look so effortless, whilst I was puffing away. I managed to maintain the same pace on the run which was encouraging, and I wasn't feeling the heat, yet.

Everything was going fine until the last lap, by which time the inevitable happened and I began to feel the sun's rays baking my shoulders. My HR dropped a few beats and as I slowed, disaster – *'oxford tri bloke'* came past. Noooooooo! I tried to stay with him, but he being the archetypal super lean aerobic triathlete, was just too fast for me. I carried on chasing him, trying to use him to drag me along and maybe get a sub 2½ hour time which was my best case scenario. With the finish line in sight I knew the 2 hours and 30 minutes best case race time wasn't going to happen. I came across the line in 2hrs 37mins, with a run time of 47 minutes and as I walked through the finish funnel I realised I was actually about to melt.

A fire engine had set up a hose that was shooting water over the finishers. It was freezing cold but exactly what I needed. I stood under it for what seemed like half an hour and caught my breath. I forced myself away from the hose (*it puts the lotion on its skin or it gets the hose again…*) and found Amy. We ambled over to the car whilst I gave another quick race debrief, which again consisted mainly of yet another swim disaster. Whilst I towelled dry at the car, Amy gave me her account of the race from a spectator's point of view, which was mainly about the spectacular collisions and falls at the bike in/out. By this time I'd totally recovered from the race, which again immediately started the 'fear' that I hadn't gone hard enough. I knew the point of all my Ironman training was to feel like I could do it all again 15 minutes after finishing, but it didn't stop the nagging at the back of my mind that I could've and should've gone faster. We set off on the hour long cool down run, by this time though the heat was incredible and was above 30°. Rather than fry my shoulders and head any more we opted for a 45 minute run around the castle grounds while the race continued into the day.

We got back to transition and I went to collect my bike. The guys either side of me on the rack were also there collecting their bikes and race gear. They were both chubby and looked completely out of shape, but their bikes were amazing. Full carbon racing machines, with Aero wheels and dripping in Dura-Ace bling. One of them asked how I got on. I told them my finish time. When he told me he'd finished at almost the same time I nearly dropped my bike. How in the name of arse had this pasty white, fat bloke done it in the same time as me? Granted, I was also a pasty white, fat AND bald bloke, but even so...my swim was crap, but my bike was OK and run was OK...surely I'd done enough to beat this guy in? Was he lying? I was obviously a lot more crap than I thought I was. He walked off with his bike clicking menacingly next to him, and I'm sure it was smirking at me......

I met up with Kiddle in Windsor in the afternoon. He'd been let out of the nursing home for the day. I went through the race with him and ever the good coach, he was telling me that it was a good first effort, etc. I told him about the guys next to me who'd out-biked me. He said that, yes, a trick bike could make a massive difference, but you still needed fast legs to move a fast bike. Even so, with the same fitness level you could expect to make up 10 minutes over 25 miles if your bike was trick enough. Yes, the guys' bikes were extremely trick. He told me not to worry and that at my first season I should just concentrate on gaining experience, speed would come next season after I'd got IM out of the way.

Yes, don't think about the trick bike...........

Chapter 11

Windsor, another aftermath...

We got back to Manchester and just as with Eton, the demons descended the next day. I went online and again began scouring the results. I found *'chubby bloke with trick bike'* and discovered that we indeed did finish more or less at the same time. He'd finished the bike almost ten minutes faster than me! I'd made this deficit up on the run, hence finishing at a similar time.

Had I done the swim in 25 minutes and the bike in 1hr 5mins I would've been on for a 2hr 20minute time! But I was doing this for race experience, not to blast out a fast time, and I had no speed in my legs anyway, just endurance. How many people went running for an hour straight after finishing? But I couldn't stop myself from feeling disappointed again, especially with another diabolical swim effort on my part. If a 2 hr 20 minute time was possible then I should've done it, but I didn't so I promptly continued to beat myself up over it. In an act of desperation mainly born out of injured pride I decided I had to get a new bike. I was about to become someone with all the gear, but no idea.

The open water swimming also had to be dealt with - losing 5-7 minutes just isn't acceptable and being slower in open water than in a 25m pool is just plain wrong. I'm more than happy to be beaten by faster people, in fact I enjoyed trying to keep with the fast guys on the bike, looking at their riding style, their position and trying to learn something from them. Watching an elite or a top amateur in action just feet away from you is the best seat in the house. But I didn't like slower people beating me. Blinded by ego, I couldn't see it wasn't about winning or losing, it was just down to experience – or lack of, on my part. Kiddle explained to me that this was the nature of multi-sport - some people are exceptionally good at a particular discipline, despite what they may 'look' like - never judge a book by its cover. Even so, I'd fallen short of my own expectations and looked forward to putting things right at Salford, but I wasn't taking it too seriously or anything…. Now to get that new bike…..

I had to go about this carefully, there had to be a plan. Sure I could simply go out and buy a bike, but that really wasn't going to go down well with Amy. Fortunately for me, I didn't have to make a plan, as Amy announced she was interested in triathlon. Being a triathlon widow was boring, she was fed up with her own training regime and wanted a change. She liked the look of triathlon. Having been to two races where she'd seen the shape and size of some of the women competing, she realised it was a sport for all abilities. I'd told Amy in the past that she'd be good at triathlon. She was already an OK swimmer and had a 10km time of sub 39 minutes. Without hesitating, I entered her into the sprint triathlon at the ITU race in Salford for the end of July. I'd be racing the same day in the OD. All we had to do now was get all her gear, and it just so happened to be her birthday. I 'fessed up about wanting a new bike, etc. She was cool about it and told me to get the bike I wanted, not to get an upgrade from what I currently had, but get the ultimate race bike that would never need changing.

I went down to the bike shop where I'd been heavily investing in everything. They had a lovely Specialized *'Transition'* triathlon specific bike ready to go. It was £1500 – could I justify this expense? Surely my trusty Renny was good enough, couldn't I just train harder to make up the time deficit? But why not train harder *and* get a new bike? I'd slash huge amounts of time off the bike leg, and over Ironman distance this could be a considerable time or energy saving move. I'm extremely good at convincing myself to spend money, and I was having no trouble talking myself into buying this bike. I asked in the shop if they'd upgrade all the components on it to *Dura-Ace* and how much that would be. Rather than do that, they advised me to buy the Transition frameset and add the Dura-Ace. This came in at a whopping £2800. Rather than do that, they suggested building one from scratch, buying each component in, including the frameset, which was a better quality carbon and aluminium – or so they said.

But something was wrong. The lad insisted that the frameset was different to the one already made up in the shop. It was supposed to be a different higher 'grade' aluminium used in the frame with better quality carbon in the forks and seat post. But that didn't make sense. I called Specialized in the UK who told me that they were in fact identical. I rang the shop back and we started the process again. They assured me I could use it for Ironman and it wouldn't cripple me. We went back to plan A with them 'buying' the components off the existing bike and replacing it with Dura-Ace. We went through it again using 'Ultegra' and for some reason this worked out £200 more expensive than building it from scratch!? Again we went through it and this time it came back at £2400. I already had some carbon *Aero-Design* tri bars, so why didn't they use them instead of charging me £100 for some new ones? They insisted that it was 'easier' that way. I asked what the difference would feel like to me, using Ultegra as opposed to Dura-Ace, and they insisted it was like night and day. None the wiser, I went for it and paid my £170 deposit.

The next day I was away with work. On the way home I passed a new bike shop on the M6 toll road called 'Bridgtown Cycles'. For some reason I called in. What a great shop! I went upstairs and began drooling on the £6000 Trek bikes – they were amazing. It's a family run shop and the son (Mike) came up and asked what I was looking for. I explained about Ironman and that my budget was around £2000, he said for that money a *Trek Madone* full carbon was the job and he'd do it for £1700! I'd already paid my deposit on the Specialized at the shop in town. What was I going to do? I took a brochure from the guy (Mike) and he probably thought he'd never see me again.

When I got home I looked at what I was really getting for the Specialized compared to the Trek, and it was a lot of money for a bike that wasn't even full carbon, it was aluminium with carbon forks and seat post. I compared the geometry of my LeMonde Reno to the Specialized and it was a much more extreme time trial orientated geometry on the Specialized. Something I wasn't used to and something that would *definitely* cripple me on Ironman. I was pretty pissed off, I'd told them what I wanted it for – why didn't they say it might not be suitable for Ironman? And they'd tried to sell me the frameset, telling me it was totally different from the made up bike in the shop, when it was in fact identical. As I thumbed through the Trek brochure from Bridgtown Bikes it fell open on a page, as simultaneously a huge fan fare sounded! It was – the *'blade....'*

It was the *Trek Equinox 11* triathlon bike. It was a full carbon, aero framed, mean looking bit of tackle. A quick check of the stats showed that despite being a triathlon specific bike, it had geometry almost identical to my LeMonde! It was £2500 – but it looked the business. I called Bridgtown Cycles and spoke to Mike again. He informed me that, yes, it would do for Ironman and yes, the Specialized would cripple me. He also told me that Trek had sold out of the Equinox 11 for 2006. Noooooooooooooooooooooooo!

But all was not lost, he had all the bits in the workshop to build one. The frame on the Equinox 11 is identical to the frame used on the Trek Team Time Trial, which good old Lance used for the time trials on the Tour de France. I just needed to give him a few days to build it. I also asked him about the difference in Dura-Ace and Ultegra. He said if you're an elite then yes, you'd notice and the small weight saving is worth it, but for me I wouldn't notice a thing. I told him to get on it!

I called the shop to let them know I was binning off the Specialized. It didn't go down well, as they wanted me to pay £35 shipping for the frame they'd ordered (the one that was *exactly* the same as the one in the shop and had no need to be ordered), plus £50 towards the time spent working out all the different options I wanted. So not only had they tried to sell me a bike on the premise that it was totally different, which it wasn't, they'd also sold me a bike unsuitable for Ironman. I agreed to pay the £35 just for an easy life. I'll never go back there and made every effort to tell as many people as possible to stay away from them. This could've been difficult, as they were the only cycling shop in Manchester, but thankfully another one has opened in the form of 'Evans'.

Moral of the story is research, research, research. I thought I knew a bit about bikes, whereas in reality I knew nothing. I also threw myself into the first half decent bike I saw instead of shopping around. If the people that work in the bike shop are all wearing jeans halfway down their arse, belts with studs on, chains hanging off them and a 'My Chemical Romance' t-shirt, chances are they're not really going to be up to speed on Ironman or triathlon specific stuff, but probably exactly who you would want to speak to about anything BMX or mountain bike related. You need a triathlon shop and there aren't that many of them around but it's definitely worth a journey to go to one.

I got a call from Mike at Bridgtown. He wanted to know if I wanted Dura-Ace brake lever/gear change (STI's) or Ultegra. I asked what the difference was, and besides nearly £100 it was just a few grams in weight. I told them to put Ultegra on, I'd just blow my nose before getting on the bike and save the weight that way. They were really helpful, and offered me all the advice I needed. Mike's sister was the record holder for riding from John o' Groats to Lands End non stop and was an accomplished time trialist, so they knew what they were talking about and all about Ironman. The were doing my bike for £2400, a saving of £100 on retail, as I was having road drop down bars on instead of the aero cow horns and bar end shifters it came with. Full aero bars are OK if you're used to them, but I wasn't and for my level of ability they advised me to go for normal road drop downs. It was having a Dura-Ace rear mech, Bontrager Carbon crank with Ultegra brakes/levers/gears and an Arione tri seat – which if it's good enough for Faris Al Sultan, the 2005 Ironman World Champ, it's good enough for me!

A quick call to the Rickster informed him I was buying a new bike. He laughed out loud, especially when I told him I wouldn't need to upgrade past this bike. He said he'd remind me of that fact in a couple of years. Well, I suppose there is the Trek Team Time Trial with full Dura-Ace, carbon wheels…..

Chapter 12

The Rickster's big day

I'd been so busy being wrapped up in my own triathlon drama, I'd forgotten that Rick had the Chester tri to do. He was supposed to do a sprint tri beforehand, but an unscheduled work drama meant he had to miss it. So his first triathlon was to be an Olympic distance! Unfortunately for Rick his training hadn't gone quite as planned, and whilst I thought my open water swimming was bobbins, Rick was still struggling in the pool. We'd done a session together in the Aquatic centre a couple of months previously – he was terrible. I thought I was inefficient, but Rick made me look like a shark.

I'd followed coach Kiddle's instructions exactly, and carried out all drills as prescribed. Drills are OK to a point, but there is an element of getting really good at being crap by doing them. Rick however hadn't followed any of the instructions or drills and had just made it up as he went along. This was why six months later he was hardly any better than that first day in the pool in Maidenhead. But this is the Rickster! He was a tonne fitter but had just gotten really good at being bad, like me.

Race morning arrived and I managed to sleep in. I drove down to Chester without really knowing where the triathlon was exactly. But if Windsor was anything to go by it wouldn't be hard to find. I was wrong. Chester at 8am in the morning was dead. I was beginning to think I'd got the wrong town! I couldn't see any sight or sound of a full Olympic distance triathlon anywhere. I drove round the centre of Chester, expecting to pick up a sign warning of cyclists or a 'road closure due to sporting event', but nothing. Driving next to the park I could see some people running in it, but there didn't seem to be that many and it could've been a small running club. As I looked on I noticed some of them in tri-suits and race numbers. Yes, that must be part of the run route, but where were all the other competitors and spectators?

I found my way round to the other side of the park and parked the car. A marshal pointed me in the direction of the finish area next to transition which took me along the run route – a path still open to the public! I didn't realise this until someone came puffing past in a tri-suit. I hastily got to the side of the path and out of the way. Looking back I could see families out for Sunday walks with pushchairs and dogs, etc, with competitors making their way around them. Whose bright idea was it to have this run route open to the public? Last thing you need on a 10km run after cycling 25 miles and swimming 1500m in a river is to trip over Bob and Vera as they saunter along the banks of the river Dee, or have some mental border collie trying to bite your ankles off. I got to transition and was struck by how small and poorly attended it was. Clearly the town wasn't behind this event, as at Windsor. It was a bit of a let down, frankly. I hoped Rick wasn't.

I found the rest of the gang who had come to support Rick. He'd done the swim and was still out on the cycle. I realised as we waited by the dismount area to cheer him on that this was the first triathlon I'd spectated at! With my illustrious triathlon career stretching to one sprint distance and one OD so far, I was actually watching one! Amateur multisport has to be the most interesting thing to watch. I love it for the people who are trying their hardest and I've nothing but praise for them. I love it for the fat blokes who think they're on the fringes of the GB team, but are as far away from that as I am. You can't beat it.

As I marvelled at the mixed bag of abilities on display, and stopped counting the number of people who fell off, still clipped into their pedals, suddenly the Rickster appeared! We all gave a massive cheer as he jogged past. He looked OK to me, he looked fresh which was a good sign. I jogged down to the fence to shout encouragement. I started to shout stuff but my voice trailed off as I watched him run around transition, looking for his rack position. All my transition advice had been ignored and he was doing it Rick style, making it up as he went along! Yeah, baby! This was great to watch and I would've been disappointed, had it been any other way.

Once he'd found his spot on the rack he chucked his bike on and sat down! Then he took his shoes off, got his socks on, got his trainers on, tied his laces, had a look around and had a crack with the race staff! This was brilliant, I was half expecting him to get a flask out and have a cup of tea with some nice digestives to dunk in it. He was doing it his way - no flapping like a headless chicken, as I'd done. With everything in order he set off on the 10km run. We all gave him a massive cheer. Rick is not a bad runner and I reckoned on a 50 minute 10km for him, so as that time approached, we made our way to the finish line. The Rickster appeared at the bottom of the field where transition was, with a massive smile on his face! He ran up waving his arms across the line in 3½ hours with a huge smile on his face. The time didn't matter – I was really really pleased for him. He got his finisher's t-shirt (which I advised him to put in the bin, so he wouldn't be tempted to wear it at another triathlon). He'd done it, his first triathlon and a full Olympic distance at that.

He gave me a quick debrief of the race. The swim had taken him 45 minutes as he'd had to breaststroke all the way (sounds familiar). He then got to transition and took his sweet time, even stopping to towel himself dry! Having being talked up by me to expect a big lift from the crowd, there were no crowds and he only saw a few people on the bike course, which were fast guys overtaking him. He was on his own for so long on the bike, he actually asked one of the marshals if he was going the right way. The bike was lonely and not the competitive race he was hoping for.

The run course took him through the park, again all on his own, before coming down the path I'd walked down to the finish. He was pleased and I was pleased for him, he said he was going to do a tri and he'd done one. Rick's not the sort of person to pour over the results and obsess where he can save time like me. I knew I'd turned into a triathlon geek. He'd done it, to do it. He was doing Salford at the end of July though, and he was determined to sort the open water swimming out. I pointed out to him that I'd had two go's so far and still managed to cock it up, despite following a comprehensive swim programme, so to complete the swim as he did was a great achievement. The whole thing was impressive really, his first triathlon had been a full Olympic Distance – no sprint triathlons to ease himself into it, straight into the full one and all self trained.

We arranged to meet at Deansgate Locks to celebrate later that afternoon. I headed back to Manchester for a two hour run on the tow path and a dust up with the mad geese.

Northern Ireland early 90's – A bit chunkier in those days

Somewhere in North Carolina 1996 – It was OK apart from the snakes and spiders.

Fort Bragg 1996 – Working with the American 82nd Airborne Division, I appear to have a C141 Starlifter balanced on my head. I've got American parachute equipment on, about to do my 1st jump using it. I liked the reserve parachute across my front with the handle on the right side - good for me as I'm right handed. Not so good if you're left handed.

Our wedding, New Years Eve, Las Vegas 2003 – If you're going to do it in Vegas there's only ONE way to do it – Elvis baby

BSB Knockhill 2005 – Jonathan on the front row with factory Honda rider (eventual 2006 BSB champ), Kiyo and defending 2004 BSB champion, John Reynolds on the Suzuki. Jonathan's racing career nearly ended here the previous year in a crash which resulted in him having a 16" pin inserted into his smashed femur. Just two seasons later it would be Jonathan on Pole at this track on the factory bike, and taking the double race win.

BSB Snetterton 2005 – Chris Jones celebrates a win in the 125cc class, just fourteen years old but he had the heart of a lion.

Irish Racer awards 2005 – Eugene, Chris and Jonathan – great lads to work with.

BSB 2005 - Jonathan often confused what he was supposed to ride.

BSB Brands Hatch 2005 – Jason Gardener, myself and Jonathan. Jason is a big bike fan and loved coming to the races, especially for the abuse he used to get from me!

European Tour – Trying to look like I know what I'm doing. If you look like you know what you're doing, people assume you do. One day I'll get found out.

European Tour – Working with Paul Casey. I'm about to get a 5kg jelly ball in the stomach at 40mph. Fortunately, my considerable padding of blubber will protect me.

Royal Windsor 2006 - Aqua-ruck in full flow – I'm the one in the wetsuit.

Royal Windsor 2006 – Another swim debacle over.

Chapter 13

To shave or not to shave?

As Salford approached I immersed myself even more into the world of triathlon, becoming more of a geek every day. I may have vaguely sorted the mental demons with training and family, but I continued to pour over race results and dream up race scenarios, possible outcomes and search through the internet for any info I might find useful. Especially anything that might say you didn't need to train for Ironman at all.

My weight loss was considerable by now, I'd gone from 94kg's to 85kg's and falling. My 1RM on bench had gone from 150kg's to picking Lilly-Mae up and none of my clothes fitted me. People who hadn't seen me for a while had to look twice. I should've taken a picture of myself at the fitness testing with Kiddle and one the day before Ironman, as my weight eventually went down to 80kgs, I bet the visual comparison of the 14kg weight loss would've been scary!

Another issue was body hair. Up until this point I was like a monkey, but I had clocked the fact that all the guys were hairless who were competing in triathlon. Not just the tanned lean fit ones, but the fat, pasty white ones as well, which gave them the appearance of overweight babies. Kiddle still insisted on removing his body hair, despite having knees made of cheese so he couldn't run anymore - the by product of years of triathlon and Ironman. He said it was the thing to do, and I'd feel better in the water. I wasn't convinced. Simply shaving all your body hair off didn't seem right. Besides I didn't think shaving would actually do the trick and surely the stubble rash would be crippling? After a discussion with Amy we decided on hair removal cream. Waxing was briefly brought up, but I'd been down that route with my chest some years before and I'd nearly pissed my pants with the pain, much to the delight of the female therapist. Some more investigating revealed that Immac (or Veet as it's now known...) actually did a bloke-specific cream. Amy was dispatched to Boots to get a supply – I was too embarrassed!

Amy returned and duly covered me in what smelt like bleach. It said on the bottle to leave it on for 4-6 minutes so I left it on for ten minutes just to be sure. My arse started burning so I knew it was time to jump in the shower! With all the hair gone it felt extremely strange, I felt like some pre-pubescent 12 year old. It was all a bit odd. But seeing as every triathlete was like it, I felt I was beginning to fit in. I couldn't bring myself to go all the way with the pubic hair as some guys do, that's just to close too wearing butt-less leather chaps as far as I'm concerned. I have to admit though I did feel faster in the pool. Obviously this was purely psychological, but if you think you're going to be faster then you probably will be.

I'd also managed to start making it down to Salford Quays for the open water swim sessions. The water sports centre is open for the idiots that want to swim in Salford Quays from May till September. It's a straightforward 400m square, and the sessions go from 6.30pm to 7.30pm initially but extend to 8.30pm as the nights get lighter. So a full two hours is plenty. Voluntarily swimming in Salford Quays wasn't something I ever imagined myself doing, but it is suitable for 'bathing' (whatever that means) and meets whatever standards it's supposed to. As I was now hairless, I fitted in a bit better in the changing rooms at the water sport centre, no longer the hairy monkey outcast. My smooth body clearly illustrated that I was a triathlete to be reckoned with, along with my 'Ironman' wetsuit. The fact that I'd only done two tri's up until that point was neither here nor there.

The swim sessions in Salford were invaluable actually, I could gauge how fast I should be swimming for 1500m in open water and soon I'd be doing IM distance in the 25m pool as well as the Quays. It was a lot less boring than the pool and you certainly didn't swallow any of the water! It also gave me the opportunity to draft, or at least experiment with drafting. I tried drafting a lot in those swim sessions, but I couldn't find the person who was just that bit faster than me. They were either too slow or way too fast, you need someone whose just that bit faster, to make it work. Ultimately I wouldn't draft anyone come Ironman, it was easier and safer to swim in 'clear' water. There was another key reason I didn't draft anyone at IM. Why, comes later.

The open water swim sessions also gave me plenty of time to practice navigating. There aren't any nice lines telling you which way to go, as there are in a pool, and you have to incorporate 'sighting' into your stroke. I hadn't needed to do this for Eton or Windsor, as I hadn't swam crawl, and on the return leg of Windsor I had the bank to tell me I was going the right way. The more confident you get the less you have to sight. I was lucky as I was a naturally 'straight' swimmer, meaning I didn't veer off course too much anyway, otherwise it would've been a nightmare. That was the one thing I practised most in the Quays, perfecting a seamless 'sighting' stroke. By the time IM came around I'd got it down to a fine art, probably saving myself a considerable amount of time.

Chapter 14

The 'blade lives

I got the call, I could go and pick my bike up. We all jumped in the car for a family trip to Bridgtown Bikes on the M6 toll. We arrived at the shop, and the spend-fest commenced. Firstly my bike was wheeled out of the workshop – it was a work of art. It just oozed speed, 'that's a real racing blade' was one comment. Yes, blade indeed – in fact that was going to be its name, the *'blade*. Do not disrespect the 'blade or it will cut you bad...... Everything about it was designed to go fast, everything on it was 'aero', even the cabling for the brakes and gears ran internally in the frame to reduce drag. This gave it exactly what it implied, a 'blade-like' appearance designed to cut through the air. I couldn't wait to ride it or race it, even though me riding it was like putting diesel in a Ferrari.

Hairless, and with a carbon bike - just like Anakin Skywalker - my conversion to the dark side was almost complete. As I 'oooohd' and 'aaaahd' over my bike, Amy was upstairs choosing hers. She'd gone for a *Scott* full carbon, which was as much to do with its colour as to how good a bike it was (chicks!). Amy decided that as I was naming my bikes she should name hers. She called it 'Barbara' or 'Babs' for short. It was £1700 but there was no point in getting her a bike she was going to need to change in the future, so might as well dive in there feet first with some top drawer tackle. She got everything from them, as they did triathlon gear, tri-suit, wetsuit, race belt, etc. This was all to prove a catastrophic (and very expensive) mistake, as it all ended up on ebay a year later. Can't live with them, can't kill them…

By the time we'd got everything including my bike, I left the shop a whopping £4000 lighter, not including the £500 deposit I'd already paid. Yes, it was turning out to be really cheap, this triathlon malarkey. We got back to Manchester and emptied everything into the flat, which had now taken on the appearance of a triathlon shop itself. I stared at the 'blade and it stared back. Tomorrow we'd go out for our first ride. It was meant to be a six hour ride but I cut this to three, with it being a new bike and simply trying it out. Any excuse to bin a long ride off!

The next morning I awoke and 'clicked' down the corridor with the 'blade. I was extremely excited, a bit too excited really for what was just a bike ride. But when you're this far over to the dark side, that's what gets you excited. I'd picked a three hour route I knew well. This was because being so intimately familiar with it on Renny meant I could make a comprehensive comparison between the two bikes.

I clipped in and set off – what a difference! This was not a bike to be messed with, it demanded maximum respect and effort. The bone shattering vibration I suffered on Renny was non-existent on the full carbon 'blade. I'd read about this in '220', how carbon absorbs all the vibration from the road, but I'd dismissed this as something only an expert could feel - on the cobble-like UK roads I doubted it made any difference at all. How wrong I was. It was silky smooth, as was everything on it. It sliced through the gears like butter.

We blasted up the A34, through Alderley Edge then out to Chelford roundabout which was the turnaround point, and already five minutes up on the same route with Renny. I blasted back down to the city centre, finishing the ride almost ten minutes quicker than usual. It was extremely impressive to ride. I stopped by the Rickster's flat to show him the 'blade. He asked if he could have a go. I told him 'the 'blade decides whether you to ride it, not the other way round.'

I got home and carefully cleaned the already clean 'blade. Even the insect population of Cheshire, which was normally splattered on the forks, etc, had given the 'blade a wide berth. Amy was pleased to hear it had gone well with the new bike. The last thing she wanted to hear was that I'd spent £2500 on a bike I didn't like. More importantly, I'd tested the riding position out. I only had to raise the seat by 1cm – other than that it was perfect. I informed Kiddle about the purchasing of the 'blade and our successful ride. He told me I had to do a five or six hour ride on it to be totally sure of no problems on Ironman. Unfortunately for Kiddle he was unaware I'd missed the first two scheduled six hour rides already, so my first long one was actually going to be on the 'blade the following week.

The problem with IM distance training rides are feed stations or lack of them - no handy race crew providing you with fresh water bottles and energy drink every fifteen miles. You have to take it all with you, and for a six hour ride that's a lot of fluid – 3.6ltrs in fact. The 'blade had space on the frame for only one bottle. Fortunately, I'd bought an aero-bottle at Windsor, an aero-dynamic water bottle that sits in between the tri bars. I'd also bought an underseat bottle cage which held two water bottles. This attaches to the seat itself where you would normally put your toolkit. I had to attach the toolkit under the bottle cage using extra Velcro, but it all worked and still looked streamlined, which is the most important thing, obviously. I now had the space for the 4ltrs or so of fluid I would need. I'd also got myself a 'bento' box, which attaches to the top tube and stem. This is a small canvas box which you can stuff with energy gels and any other treats you fancy. In my pursuit of Ironman tips, one that stood out was to have something savoury on the bike, as you apparently get sick of gels. This interested me professionally as I was a big believer in 'fatty' carbs for energy, as opposed to using simple carbs all the time. It all made sense to me, but more likely it was just a good excuse to have some sort of pastry sweet.

On the 112 miles of the bike leg on Ironman you need to get as much fuel on board as possible, to not only get through the bike but see you through the run afterwards, so this seemed like a sound piece of advice. Getting sick of gels might tempt you to stop having them at some point on the bike, which would be catastrophic in terms of energy depletion. I duly stuck a piece of buttery, soft flapjack into my bento box along with a couple of gels and an energy bar. This all had to be done very carefully so as not to upset the 'blade - I didn't want it feeling like I was using it as a pack horse.....

The day of my first long ride, and I had a 40 minute run to do afterwards. I was going to try and do the 112 miles in the six hours - that was my goal. Kiddle said the main thing was to get past the 'wall' at eighty miles - a point where people start getting off the bike to stretch and talk themselves out of finishing - but for me it was important psychologically to do IM distance, not just 6 hours in the saddle. This was going to be a tough session, six hours of riding followed by forty minutes of running. I was supposed to do an hour swim before the ride, but despite being the weekend, even I couldn't squeeze eight hours of continuous training into one day. The swim was a 'green' session anyway, meaning it wasn't a 'must do'. I thought back to my early training sessions when two hours on the bike seemed a lot. I set off on the 'blade to the start of the eighteen mile loop at Chelford roundabout some 25 miles away from our flat, a loop I was to do four times before retuning home, making the entire journey 112 miles.

Once at Chelford roundabout, I settled into my four laps. It couldn't be that bad, could it? I wasn't trying to break any world records, was I? I just had to keep it steady and within my HR limits, so as not to burn too much energy. The usually bone shattering ride along the roads was much smoother on the 'blade - something I'd already sussed anyway. British roads are shocking as we all know. What I had to keep an eye out for was potholes - another reason for doing laps on a familiar route. I'd been caught out before by a gaping 1ft hole in the road, which a car would miss as it was near to the kerb. I, however, hit it full on and thought my wheel was going to explode. This is why 'heavy' training wheels are a good idea. Hitting something like that on your trick carbon wheels probably wouldn't be a good idea. The first lap was OK, I'd done 42 miles in total and felt good. The second lap again was OK, I'd done 60 miles. Then the third lap...it wasn't OK.

At some point halfway round the third lap it felt like someone had come along with a giant syringe and sucked all the energy out of my legs. I felt fine in myself, but had no energy or strength. The slightest incline would sap all the speed out of me. This was bizarre. Then I stopped feeling fine in myself and started to crumble. My back started to ache horrendously, my shoulders were starting to freeze together and the balls of my feet were in agony. I tried to ease the pain in my feet by wriggling my toes, which was excruciating, a bit like the worst pins and needles you've ever had. As 80 miles approached, I could now see what Kiddle was talking about. Having another 32 miles to do was not doing me any favours psychologically. How was I going to cope, knowing I had to run a marathon, come race day? Had I taken on too much? The demons returned with a vengeance.

I ploughed on, trying to ease the pain in my feet and back. It wasn't working. Then a strange thing happened. I randomly started to feel better. The harder I pushed, the better my feet felt, and the pain in my back and shoulders started to subside. Starting the fourth and final lap was a real psychological boost and the more the pain subsided the faster I went, or it could've been the other way round. Soon enough it was time to turn on the return leg home, which is slightly more downhill than on the out leg. All the aches and pains had gone and suddenly the prospect of running a marathon after this didn't seem so impossible. The traffic lights were a welcome relief as I headed back into Manchester city centre. A great opportunity to unclip the feet and stretch the lower back.

I arrived back home in high spirits. I'd broken through the psychological and physical 'wall' Kiddle was talking about. I looked down at the trip computer as I got off the bike outside our building - 112 miles in 6 hours and 5 minutes. I'd done it. Standing in the flat I had a strange numb feeling in my legs as I quickly got changed. Even so, I was actually looking forward to going for a run – I thought it would 'stretch me out'. Setting off on my forty minute joggette, I plodded down the tow path at my prescribed HR. I had no trouble staying in my HR range, which would normally mean pushing it, but due to the effort and fatigue of the bike, fast jogging was all I needed to do as my body worked over time. I was in exceptionally high spirits. Even the prospect of a scrum down with the psycho geese further along the tow path didn't bother me.

The psychological 'win' of doing IM distance was one of the single most important sessions I did, and would do again a few times before race day. Do not make the mistake of leaving it until the day. You do not want any surprises on race day. You'll spot the people that have - they're pushing their bikes back to transition instead of starting the last lap.

Chapter 15

Salford Olympic

The year marched on, as did the training and my event calendar. I had just one more triathlon to do before Ironman, Salford. This was an ITU World Cup race, which meant it was a well organised and televised event, attracting all the big names in the sport. It was also to be Amy's first triathlon on 'Babs'. The great thing about this race, though, was the fact it was ten minutes away - no driving for hours, no B&B's, just bob down the road and do the business. I knew where to park and the quickest way to registration – all that jazz that comes with local knowledge and just makes things that bit easier.

As with all OD races the registration was the day before at a hotel down by the Quays. We loaded the 'blade and Babs onto the car and off we rocked to register. Registration was a straightforward affair and we were both through it in no time. A quick rendezvous with the Rickster to talk about race day, then round to transition to rack our bikes.

Something I hadn't thought about was having to leave the 'blade in transition overnight *in Salford*.

There aren't many occasions I can think of when you'd leave thousands of pounds worth of bikes in Salford all night in plain view, but this is what we were all doing. Racking the 'blade amongst the other trick carbon bikes made me feel a bit more of a triathlete than my previous outings, even though the purchase of the 'blade was a clear case of getting my intentions confused with my abilities. Looking up revealed a darkening sky with some ominous looking clouds. Glancing round transition, I could see plenty of people had covered their bikes in bin liners in case it rained in the night. How could I have forgotten something so simple? I hoped it wouldn't rain - I knew the 'blade would not appreciate being left out all night in it. As we left for home a torrential downpour of biblical proportions started. The 'blade wasn't going to be happy.....

Race morning was the usual comedic early start to get breakfast in. I also had the Rickster to pick up en route. Amy's race didn't start till 9.30am so she was going to make her own way down. I picked the Rickster up and the anticipation about the race was almost palpable in the car. We parked up and made our way to transition. I wasn't sure where the swim entry, bike exit was. etc, so it's always worth a recce. Having left the 'blade in transition overnight in Salford Quays, I was relieved to see it still there race morning at 6am, as opposed to being liberated by a group of 11yr olds on ASBO's during the night. However, the 'blade looked extremely unimpressed at being left all night in the rain.

I spent the next twenty minutes faffing unnecessarily with

my stuff before deciding all was in order. This is always an awkward time for me - do I get changed into my wetsuit now, or is it too early? Wait another ten minutes? I tended to spend too much time watching what others were doing instead of sticking to my own plan I felt comfortable with, but you don't want to look like a clueless gimp, do you? Which I probably did anyway with all the faffing around. A quick RV with the Rickster to shake hands and wish each other luck, then it really was time to get changed. This time I remembered to squeeze my shoulder blades together when my suit was zipped up and didn't try and strangle myself with the velcro.

We all made our way to the swim start, which was the usual deep water job following two laps of the quay. There were a number of things that were playing on my mind about this swim start. Everyone under the age of 39 was starting at the same time, as opposed to waves. This meant 250 of us would be thrashing around at the start. With this in mind I knew the usual 'aqua-ruck' would now become 'aqua kill or be killed'.

After being kept waiting for 15 minutes we were eventually told to get into the water and line up. Whilst chatting to a couple of fellow 'soon to be ruck-ees' in the water, a klaxon was sounded. Looking round confused (nothing new for me there, then) we looked at each other and asked if that was the start. Judging by the fact that almost everyone was hammering up the quays without us, it was safe to assume this was the case (where was the ten minute warm up and swim brief..?) Now in a state of blind panic, I thrashed wildly into a group of swimmers, determined to put a good swim in after my last two outings. My mind set was 'everyone in my way must die'. Unfortunately for me I wasn't the only one thinking that, as I had my goggles and hat pulled off. Coughing and spluttering, I had to try and put them back on whilst treading water. By the time I'd done this, I was dead last.......great.

A bizarre thought entered my head, involving the mad towpath Canadian geese attacking everyone on my behalf, having being trained to do so at my command. Like an uber-criminal from a Bond film I'd trained them to kill. A simple press of the red button on the remote control and everyone would have a world of pain descending on them in the Quay, in the form of the demented Geese. Whilst the rest of the field was being pecked to death, I would effortlessly swim past, coming out of the water in 1st place....

However, I didn't have a flock of wild geese trained to kill on demand by remote control, so I swam on to the turn point. I actually saw the Rickster breaststroking away as I desperately tried to make up time. I briefly contemplated pulling his feet as I passed him, then thought better of it. If someone had done that to me at Eton, it would have been terminal for my race, as I would've gone into a blind panic. I ploughed on and seemed to be overtaking a lot of people, but that's not surprising when you start at the back. I felt good and was sure this was going to be a good swim effort, despite ending up dead last at the start. I stayed in clear water as opposed to trying to draft people, and soon enough the last lap came round. I thrashed to the swim exit, and as I got out of the water a quick glance at my HRM showed...I hadn't even started it. It was then a crazy 50m zig zag run up the side of the quay to transition, but instead of running straight into transition we had to run 100m in bare feet across stones, before getting to the swim entry. What I thought was the swim entry to transition on my recce was in fact the bike exit.

I'd done the UJ on the floor thing again to mark my position, and a portaloo was just to the left of my rack position, so it was dead easy to find. Unfortunately I'd left my swim hat and goggles in my hand when trying to peel my wetsuit off, meaning my hand was stuck! I then had a two minute fight with my wetsuit before getting out of it. The 'blade just ignored me. Shoes on, gel down my throat and helmet fixed, I ran through transition onto the mount area. Time to see what the 'blade could do.

The bike course was bobbins. It was a closed road (great, no pensioners in Nissan Micra's trying to mow everyone down) involving eight laps of the quays, with a hundred right angle turns and fifty roundabouts. The 'blade is a time trial bike and thrives on being let loose on open roads, not riding round Frankie and Benny's in Salford Quays. The reason for this, obviously, is television. The bike course simply rode around the landmarks of Salford Quays – Manchester United, Imperial War Museum, Lowry Theatre, etc. From the air and on television this looks extremely impressive, but in reality makes for a poor bike course.

My initial disgust at the course was soon wiped away though, as I've discovered a hitherto unknown to me amateur triathlete's Achilles heel – going round sharp bends! For whatever reason, even the 'fast' guys seem unaware that tyres have side grip. I was straight into a race with someone I named *'Aero Helmet Gobshite'* bloke and *'Warrington tri'* bloke. They powered past me on the only straight in the course, much to the 'blade's displeasure. However, as soon as we got to the tight and twisty stuff, they suddenly started riding backwards, where I simply went past them using my previous two wheel experience, trying to get my knee down on the corners. *'Aero Helmet Gobshite'* should have spent more time working on corner speed instead of slagging off slower riders in his way, a fact I pointed out as I past him round the outside on a corner. You get that a lot in Olympic distance races, surprisingly - wankers shouting and swearing at riders who are 'slowing' them down. Wearing an Aero helmet and having a fast bike doesn't mean people have to get out of your way - you ride past them. Triathlon is a sport for all abilities and this guy really wound me up by having a go at 'slower' riders.

With *'Aero Helmet Gobshite'* behind me I got into a race with *'geordie bloke'*, who had the cheek to engage in banter with me! You can't do 'banter' whilst on the 'blade! He was my saviour actually, as I'd spent the last forty minutes thriving on cutting up all the usual fast guys on the tight course, and I hadn't been counting the laps! Doh! Fortunately for me *'geordie bloke'* could count and we had just three laps to go. This was the other bad part about the bike course - having to count eight laps. I'm sure there were plenty of people who miscounted laps during the bike. Apart from scaring myself on the corners the rest of the bike was uneventful. One guy crashed in front of me on a roundabout, and another poor guy sat fixing a puncture for the last three laps of the race. I didn't even take a puncture kit, as I knew nothing would dare penetrate the 'blade's tyres. I only saw the Rickster once on the bike. I caught his huge grin coming towards me on the other side of the road. He was shouting 'don't 'diss the 'blade!' as he passed. It was great to see him having fun. I funnelled into the dismount area and jogged to my slot in the rack. Time to blast 10km out.

As I ran out of transition I realised someone had replaced my legs with ones that had been drinking all day. I'd gone a bit hard on the bike - the price was jelly legs on the run. The run was soul destroying. Four laps, mostly on a straight road running parallel to the quays and Manchester United, bringing you back over the bridge for a turnaround outside the Lowry Theatre. Again, great for TV, but not such an inspiring route to *actually* run.

After 2.5km my legs returned to normal and I settled into a good pace. I did the first 5km in 21 minutes feeling good and hopeful of a 42-3 minute 10km time. I wasn't really in a race with anyone, no-one was overtaking me and I was very slowly catching the guy in front. I prefer to be 'racing' someone rather than race the clock. This obviously takes your mind off things as you concentrate on what's going on around you. Running or racing on your own leaves you with your own thoughts. Running up and down the long straight road was tough psychologically, but as far as I was concerned, anything that was a mental test as well as physical was a good thing in preparation for Ironman.

After 8km I got a stitch, which forced me to ease off considerably. It's tempting to try and run through a stitch and control it with breathing, but you're walking a fine line between getting over it and having to stop and walk. Rather than run the risk of stopping, I knocked the pace right off, which resulted in someone overtaking me, but that's the way it goes.

With the stitch sorted, I upped the pace again. I knew a sub 42 minute 10km was off the cards now but I wanted to get in sub 45 minutes, 2 minutes quicker that Windsor. As I came across the bridge towards the Lowry Theatre for the last time I could see the finish funnel. Glancing down at my HRM (which I'd started on the bike..) I could see a sub 45 minute 10km was mine, I crossed the line, another OD race under my belt.

I wandered into transition to grab my gear and by the time I'd collected everything together, I was recovered. Which again was the main goal - to feel like I could go again. The problem with recovering so quickly is, it leaves you feeling you didn't try hard enough, yet again. I could've probably found 10 minutes by killing myself all the way round from the swim to run, which is what everyone is doing. But doing that would mean I'd be no good for the rest of the day, and Ironman is a very long day!

I left my bike and gear in transition, towelled dry and got changed into clean clothes - at least a hot shower at home was only a short drive away. I headed to the finish line drinking my recovery drink, to watch the Rickster come in and see if I could catch Amy on the bike doing her sprint distance. I was supposed to do an hour bike, but I binned it off, as an hour ride from Salford Quays is 90% stopping at traffic lights, so I didn't see the point.

As I got to the finish, the Rickster was already and covered in champagne! His parents, daughter and a group of mutual friends had all come to cheer him on and had sprayed him with champagne as he crossed the line. His goal was three hours and he'd done it! Knocking a massive 30 minutes off his previous time just a month before. His main goal of the year was over, Chester was a warm up and Salford was Rick's Ironman. He'd also managed to raise £1200 for his dad's cancer charity. The pressure was off and he could now relax, he'd achieved his triathlon goal. I could only look on enviously as my triathlon goal was still four weeks away, and finishing was in no way a definite. The Rickster had set himself the challenge and completed it. Question is, would I?

I wasn't sure what my total time was as I'd forgotten to start my HRM in the swim bollocks. As Rick went to get dried and changed, we all moved to the barriers to see if we could catch Amy. This was actually Amy's first ride on Babs! She didn't have any SPD clip in pedals on it - I'd decided that was just asking for trouble - so she just had normal peddles on. Just as I was thinking I'd missed her, she came past! It was great to see her and she looked like she was going well. The next time round she pulled in to the dismount area and was soon running back past, after what must've been a quick transition.

I waited by the turnaround point, watching the clock. I knew that she could do a sub 20 minute 5km with the pressure on in a race. As 10 minutes approached I saw her run down the finish funnel. By the time I'd spotted her she'd already crossed the line. I assumed something was wrong. I made my way across to the finish, expecting her to say she'd pulled something. No – she just didn't realise it was two laps! Classic!

With the days racing over for Team Roberts, we headed home for a much needed power shower and to get changed. We arrived back at the flat where my mum met us, as she'd been looking after Lilly-Mae all day again. We'd arranged to meet everyone at Deansgate Locks for a post race drink and food. It was a lovely summer's day and I was looking forward to well deserved ice cold shandy. As we got changed we talked through the race with each other. Amy had just turned up and bluffed it on the day, she hadn't even looked at any of the race info beforehand - bike course, run route, etc - hence not knowing the run was two laps. After the swim she ran into transition and jumped straight onto her bike and began to hammer through transition with one of the marshals frantically trying to stop her! I wish I could've seen that, it must've been hilarious!

Team Roberts made its way to Deansgate Locks and spent the rest of the afternoon relaxing in the summer sun with the rest of the gang, whilst Lilly-Mae trashed the condiment pot and anything else she could get her little hands on. The Rickster already had some of the results from the website - his bike time was the same as mine!? Eh? I nearly fell off my chair, but had to keep an air of nonchalance about it. How was it possible? I knew the bike was 1 hour 5 minutes for me as I'd started my HRM as I crossed the mount line and timing mat on the bike leg. So how had the Rickster managed to post a similar bike time to mine? I had no idea what had happened on the bike and accused Rick of taking performance enhancing drugs. I could feel the 'fear' coming. I didn't want to ruin a nice afternoon out with the family by succumbing to post race IM training demons, so a well timed shandy subdued them...for now...

Amy was listed as actually winning the sprint tri due to running a 10 minute 5km! We joked about how the BTA would be on the phone that afternoon offering her a place on the GB team. With the afternoon drawing to a close I could see the party demons gripping the Rickster. With his triathlon goals complete and living 'clean' for months I could see a very large one on the horizon for him that night. Team Roberts headed home and left the rest of the gang to begin their well deserved evening of debauchery.

As soon as we got through the door the laptop was on, and straight to the race website. Amy let out a huge sigh of boredom, as I began my usual ritual of pouring over the results. What had gone wrong on the bike? How had the Rickster got a similar time to me? As soon as the results came up I could see something was amiss. My swim time was 32:46 which included the ridiculous 50m zig zag run before crossing the timing mat. This seemed about right, as slow as it was. T1 was down as 3:09 which again was about right considering the 100m run across gravel just to get to the bike. However, my bike time was down as 57:53!? How was that possible? I'd looked at my HRM as I crossed the timing mat and it was 65:00. Then even more bizarre, T2 was 10:39!? The run was 44:29, which I knew was right.

Basically the timings were naused up and some T2 time needed adding to the bike, so Rickster's website time was similar to my true time. I let out a huge sigh of relief, the Rickster banging out a similar bike time to me at this late stage of my training was nothing short of disastrous. Months of training and the king of party animals is as fast as me. Regardless of the bizarre splits my overall time was 2 hours 28 minutes. I'd got the sub 2½ hours I wanted at a pace where I could've gone round again straight after – another huge psychological win. But not for long, the sub 2½ hour time was almost immediately pushed aside as all I could think about was the 2¼ hour time I could've got. It was Windsor all over again, but worse this time as I was supposed to be 5 weeks fitter. I gave in entirely to the IM training demons, no amount of shandy's was going to hold them off now...

Chapter 16

The swim nemesis...

With all my pre Ironman races out of the way, it was time to flap about the big day just in case I wasn't flapping about it enough already. It was just four weeks till the monster race. It was also time to get the last of the 'quality' sessions in before tapering off in the ten days before the event. I had just three long sessions of each discipline left, apart from swimming, in which I had a quite a few long ones left. I'd lost the majority of the weight I was going to lose by now, which was a whopping 13kgs. My arse, arms and pretty much everything else had disappeared, much to Amy's distaste. I was also limited to two pairs of jeans, as nothing else fit me – which meant purchasing new tops. Yet another unforeseen Ironman expense.

I used two pools for the swim training, the Aquatic Centre and our local David Lloyd gym, more so David Lloyd as it had a crèche. The Aquatic Centre had two distinct personalities – mornings and evenings. The 6.30am crowd were hard core swimmers with excellent lane discipline, you went in the 'fast lane' at your peril during these times and the pool was in 50m mode. Here 10 year olds training with the swim clubs would sail past you as if you were stood still in the next lane. They had to be part dolphin. As it got towards 8am, more of a pre-work splash-around crowd would arrive and the pool was split into two 25m secstions. After 9am it was dead, as most people were at work and the students hadn't peeled themselves off their pizza encrusted beds yet.

The evenings were the total opposite at the Aquatic Centre. It degenerated into a free for all despite, being laned off for swimming. I made the fatal error of going at 6.30pm one evening. I managed only three lengths before sacking it off after colliding with two different people who were stood in the middle of the fast lane chatting. This evening experience totally put me off the Aquatic Centre full stop and the council had changed all the parking regulations around the centre anyway, making David Lloyd the more convenient choice.

I'd done IM distance just once in the 25m pool so far, 1hr 14mins of mind numbing ,152 lengths. Can you imagine doing 152 lengths? Can you imagine trying to keep count whilst doing 152 lengths? If you're training for Ironman then you won't have to imagine as you'll have to do it at some point. I'm fairly certain I never actually did 152 lengths, I most probably did 154, 156 or something. I dreaded looking at the training schedule and seeing 'swim 12' which was IM distance. Nevertheless, I knew that it wasn't just about swimming 3.8km, it was also about the mental torture of doing it in a 25m pool. As I keep saying Ironman is all about mental torture. Just how much, I'd find out on the big day in four weeks time.

The other invaluable thing I did was use my *Aqua Sphere* goggles in the pool for IM distance, as those were the goggles I was going to use come race day. I'd used them in the swim sessions in Salford Quays, but hadn't done anything over 1500m in them. 1600m into the swim, the goggles were killing me, they were way too tight. I hadn't noticed because the problem only manifested itself after thirty minutes or so. It got so bad I had to stop and loosen them slightly. I used those goggles for every swim after that, no matter how short the session, loosening them one notch at a time till I could do an hour without feeling like I was having a brain haemorrhage. This highlighted another key point – use the kit you're going to race in and use it to death, not just the week before the race for 10 minutes at a time.

It's here at your pool of choice that you also get to instinctively know the 'type' people that you share lanes with. Being a gym means the pool isn't as busy as you'd think, but the chances of encountering the 'hard core' are slim. With the amount of time you spend swimming you get to know certain characters in the pool, and I don't just mean individuals you may see on a regular basis, but certain *'types'* of people.

As swimming is officially the amateur triathlete's worst discipline, I feel it my duty to point out the various types of people you're likely to encounter in the pool.

First up is the *'alpha-male'*. This dude is out for the sprint, not the marathon, and can be extremely irritating. After doing a weight session, this swimmer will come down to the pool and get in the fast lane, even if the pool is empty. With board shorts trailing in his wake, he thrashes down the pool as if escaping a great white shark, before taking a ten minute rest at the end. This means that he may be possibly swimming faster than you for this one length, but you're in there doing a double 30 minute session with a 5 minute break. So you have to put up with him thrashing past you, just to stop for half an hour and check out the yummy mummies going into the baby pool.

Age: Early 20's
Gender: Always male.
Body type: Slightly fat but thinks he's muscular.
Most likely to: Race you over 25m then stop for ½ an hour.
Drives: VW Golf, which will be diesel, but de-badged so you think it's a GTi, with an exhaust the size of channel tunnel
Wears: Board shorts which were bought for the annual holiday to Magaluf as opposed to Bondi Beach.

The next one is the *'other triathlete'*. You can spot these dudes a mile off due to the amount of swim accessories they have poolside. Pull-buoy, kick board, water bottle, flippers, gloves, session sheet, etc, etc. In fact everything you have! They're usually a much better swimmer than you, leaner than you and have a *'tri-suit'* tan. They may or may not speak to you, should you find yourselves at the same end of the pool in between sets, but if they do it's usually with good intentions and advice. This is mainly out of sympathy, once you tell them you're training for an Ironman.

Age: Early 30's
Gender: Usually male.
Body type: Super lean.
Most likely to: Be doing an extremely complicated swimming session, all twice as fast as you.

Drives: An estate, with bike pumps, inner-tubes and boxes of power gels strewn in the back.

Wears: Extremely dodgy swimwear which goes down well with the 'pink' crowd in the gym – more or less what you'll be wearing as well.

Next up is the most dangerous – one I named the *'swim nemesis'*. Unlike the others you won't spot the swim nemesis until it's too late. The first thing you'll know they're there is when they pass you, in the next 'slower' lane. You'll be happily swimming away in the fast lane, when from nowhere in the medium lane an older, slightly chunky lady will come sailing past you. Swim nemeses are always female, always older than late 30's and always a bit on the chunky side. Should you ever speak to one you'll find that they were a swimmer of some calibre in their younger days until getting married and having kids, etc.

The swim nemesis puts you in an awkward position. Do you stick to your pace, whilst having someone in the slower lane going faster than you? Or up the pace, compromising your endurance and ability to finish the session? The swim nemesis isn't in there for ten minutes either, they're usually in there for a good forty lengths at least. I'd been lucky with the swim nemesis, they'd be finishing a swim when I got in, or vice-versa, saving me from embarrassing myself.

Age: Late 30's, early 40's.

Gender: Always female.

Body type: Three kids might have added a few pounds, but don't be fooled…

Most likely to: Effortlessly sail past you in pool, do tumble turns with ease.

Drives: People carrier, occupied by various soft toys and 'brats on board' sticker in window.
Wears: Trusty *'Speedo'* speed suit and hat.

My first encounter with the swim nemesis was at the worst possible time, halfway through IM distance in the 25m pool. It started like any other IM distance. The first 60 lengths went by without incident, then in the other lane coming towards me...THE SWIM NEMESIS. I could tell from the rate of closure, she was going faster than me. It was the swim nemesis - it's what they do. I had maybe three lengths at most before she caught me, and the humiliation of the *'been overtaken by someone in a slower lane'*. What to do? What to do? What to do? I'm doing IM distance, I can't start pumping the lengths out as if in a sprint triathlon, can I?

I succumbed to a testosterone fuelled decision of extremely piss poor proportions, *keep ahead of the swim nemesis at all costs.* Like a WWII destroyer captain, I ordered all full ahead. However, I'd given the worst order since the CIA thought it was a good idea to arm and train the Taliban. I turned what was already a difficult swim into a nightmare. I had to make my eyes bleed as the swim nemesis relentlessly followed in the other lane, never fading, never slowing. Like a polar bear tracking its prey across the arctic wasteland, I was the doomed baby seal in its sights.

After what seemed like three hours, the 152 lengths were complete and I stabbed the *'stop'* button on my watch - 1hr 9mins. I dragged myself out of the pool feeing terrible, and continued to feel like shit for the rest of the day. Beware the swim nemesis, beware your ego and pride. Leave them at the pool side or you will be made to look like a tit, as I was. But at least I got a PB out of it.

One place I didn't encounter any nasty surprises was Salford Quays. I still enjoyed the swim sessions there, and one session left to do was IM distance in open water. I turned up for the usual Thursday night session, got changed and eased myself into the nice brown water. I made my way to the second buoy and started my HRM – just 9½ laps to do of the 400m course.

With no one around me I had to gauge my pace myself, again not a bad thing. I plodded on, trying to keep a pace I knew would keep me fresh. I tried drafting a few people again, but it was more trouble than it was worth and I spent too much time worrying about touching them, rather than just concentrating on my swimming. I tried to have sly looks at my HRM as my arm came over the top to see if I was on time. I was hitting the right pace just about, around 7 minutes per 400m lap. Swimming 2.4miles in the Quays was a much better swim experience than the 25m pool - I only had to count to 'nine' for a start. Not having to stop and turn every 25m was also a billy bonus.

As lap 9 approached I upped the pace very slightly. Crossing the last buoy I looked at my HRM – 1hr 9mins, exactly the same as my crippling time in the pool. Except this time I felt great and ready to ride 112 miles. I let myself think I was ready, albeit very briefly.

Chapter 17

One last cheeky race...

I had to squeeze one more unscheduled race in before Ironman, that being a 10 mile time trial. I had one scheduled in my training programme which happened to fall on a day when a local cycling club hold their club 10 mile time trials. Ordinarily I would just simply smash a time trial out on my own, dicing with traffic within a 2 hour session, so I was looking forward to an actual race. I went on the website for any info for 'newbies' and with directions noted, I went upstairs to inform the 'blade of the evening's plans. The 'blade as usual showed no emotion.

With the 'blade loaded up on the roof rack, I set off in search of race registration, which was situated *'halfway down Blah Blah Lane, just past the lay-by'*. Despite these sketchy directions which sounded more like they belonged on a 'dogging' website, I managed to find the lane. Actually I didn't, some bloke in a Porsche 4x4 came past with £6k worth of TT bike on the roof, I followed him and as suspected, we were heading to the same time trial.

Arriving at race registration I discovered an even more bizarre set of people than amateur triathletes. I parked next to *'Porsche bloke'*. I could see the 'blade making a mental note to 'cut him bad' when the race got underway, I just didn't want to make a tit of myself. After registering and picking my race number up (11, meaning I was 11th to set off, as I found out whilst making a tit of myself...) I set off on a pre-race warm up.

With the 7.15pm race start time approaching, I made my way to the start and thought I'd get to the front. It was here the starter explained I was 11th to start, and riders start in number order at one minute intervals...doh! I laughed out loud and said I knew that, and was simply trying to set a world record time. No one else laughed.

As I waited the 11 minutes till my start, I had time to check everyone out. It was a spectacular display of blubber in 'too tight lycra', with helmets straight off the set of 'Star Trek' combined with seriously expensive bikes, some very serious athletes who looked fast even when stationary, and myself. One of the extremely serious riders would be just one minute behind me, no12. I had to keep no12 behind me - the 'blade would not be happy if he caught and overtook me.

I noticed a mood shift in the 'blade - *'Porsche bloke'* had arrived, chopsing off about the previous week's racing, and the one before that, and the one before that, etc, etc – you get the picture. The 'blade was praying for him to be no10, just one minute in front of me, so it could take him. He was no3! Was it possible? Could we make up eight minutes in 10 miles? The 'blade seemed to think so, despite the almost gale force winds. I also noticed no10 wearing a time trial suit with more hair than a silver back gorilla sprouting out of it in all directions. This is what I probably would've looked like, were it not for *Veet*. This bloke obviously still liked feeling like a 'bloke' rather than the 12 year old I did.

It was my time to go, and after being counted down from thirty seconds, I rocketed off. There's a great hare and hounds element to time trialing. I was killing myself so the 'blade could take the people in front, but I was also trying to keep the very serious time trialist, who was behind me and wearing sponsored team kit, from catching me. After less than 1½ miles I could see *'hairy bloke'*. Was he riding in the granny gear? He must be, for me to be catching him so soon. I was over pedalling and working anaerobically, but it was only 10 miles, not the 100 mile death rides I'd being doing. I kept glancing behind me - no sign of *'serious bloke'*. After two miles I'd caught *'hairy bloke'* on a down hill part. With 38mph showing on the computer I flew past him, shouting 'track' because he decided to ride in the middle of the road, or maybe the drag from his body hair was pulling him to the right and slowing him down? Still no sign of the guy who set off one minute behind me. Could I actually hold him off? I doubted it. The wind was horrendous, and the 'blade (like all aero frame bikes) did not like it. It gets sucked around in the direction of the wind, not good when travelling at pace with HGV's coming in the opposite direction.

A quick glance behind and in sight was the serious time trialist! I couldn't go any faster and the inevitable happened - he came past and gracefully pulled away. Trying to keep up with him, I almost forgot about *'Porsche bloke'* until he came past in the opposite direction. He was 1½ mile in front. Could I do it? I managed to keep the fast guy in sight till turnaround point, which was a small roundabout. Once onto the return leg he easily pulled away and there was no way I could keep with him. I envied the ease with which he seemed to generate speed. I managed to pass two more people somehow and found myself wishing there were more miles, as the 10 mile point rapidly approached. Then, in a straight part of the road... PORSCHE BLOKE WAS IN SIGHT.

I was in a state of panic - 'Porsche bloke' was in real danger of finishing before I caught him. By now my legs were burning and my lungs had that horrendous 'phlegmy' taste you get if you run hard on an ice cold morning. With just ½ mile to go he was looming large in the scope, the 'blade could smell the kill and I wasn't allowed to ease off. I was also in with a 25 minute finish. But...disaster...he crossed the line just in front of me, with the first drops of what ended up being a torrential downpour beginning to fall. I was gutted, the 'blade ignored me and my 25 minute finish had slumped to 26.05.

It wasn't all bad news, I was overtaken by only that one guy, and 26.05 in horrendous windy conditions ain't that bad. It was good to do a 'pure' time trial, but I should've ridden there and ridden home really. Not very 'Ironman', driving up there. I didn't feel too bad though, I'd rather the rain was bouncing off my windscreen during the 20 mile journey home than my face! For once the post race fear didn't come on and despite allowing myself some credit, the IM training demons didn't descend on me for some reason.

Chapter 18

It's party time

August arrived and with it a twenty day countdown to IM, but first the small matter of Lilly-Mae's birthday party. I was by now super stressed out about Ironman (as if it was possible to get more stressed out?), and wanting to make my daughter's first birthday special. We hadn't decided anything about the party - where, when, etc. Did we have it on the actual day? Or after Ironman? Should we simply have it in the flat with just family, or somewhere else and invite friends? In town or out of town? Amy managed to pin me down and drag me away from staring at my training schedule on the cupboard door, to finally get the little dude's birthday sorted.

The location was *'Croma'* in town - a great pizza restaurant with plenty of room in the back for everyone, not the non-descript coastal town in East Anglia. We were going to have it on Lilly-Mae's actual birthday, in the middle of the afternoon, which restricted numbers, but that wasn't a bad thing. It was also going to be a 'pink' party, meaning everyone had to wear pink, no exceptions!

All we had to do now was sort a cake, which is easier said than done. After some scouting around we found a bakers called 'Slatteries' in Prestwich. I'm not into 'cakes' but this place was unbelievable. I didn't realise it was possible to actually make cakes into the things they had on display. When I asked what the limit was, the response was, how much you were prepared to spend. Lilly-Mae's favourite TV programme was the *'Jammers'* on Baby TV. Amy took a picture of them with a digital camera and showed it to Slatteries – it wouldn't be a problem to make a *'Jammers'* cake. Sorted. The good thing about the party was I could knock myself out on cake as it was Ironman week, so carbs were all good!

The training went on and for the last two weeks or so before race day, I began to 'taper'. This meant quite a sever reduction in volume, but the intensity was ramped up. I was doing short, sharp sessions again, something I'd not done for months. It was perfect. I felt the sessions were doing exactly what they were supposed to – sharpen me up. It was also nice to do some almost anaerobic sessions again after being *aerobic lord* for nine months. I went through some stats. I'd lost 13kgs, cycled over 2500 miles and swum hundreds of miles in the nine months I'd been training for Ironman. I'd also done no more than 60% of the programmed sessions. But it doesn't matter how much training you do, you never ever feel it's enough anyway. I finished the last of my 'long' training with IM distance in Salford Quays, keeping it steady and at a pace I felt I could get out and cycle 112 miles, followed by running 26.2 miles. I finished the swim in 1hr 9mins again, fresh as a daisy and ready to ride 112 miles. Although if you did put a daisy in Salford Quays, I seriously doubt it would come out in any condition that could be described as 'fresh'.

The day of Lilly-Mae's birthday arrived, and it went perfectly. I went to pick the cake up and nearly had a heart attack. We'd massively over-estimated how big the cake needed to be. As the *Jammers* are musical instruments, the original plan was to have the 'drum' as a cake (already being cake shaped) and the other characters made out of sugar. The baker told us it would feed 50, but we'd decided that it wouldn't be 50 'Team Roberts portions' and asked them for the 'piano' to be made into a cake as well as the drum. It was the size of a small coffee table and weighed nearly as much, the icing on the cakes nearly an inch thick. The enamel on my teeth started to peel off, just looking at it. This was the cake equivalent of weapons grade plutonium. All I had to do now was get in into the car without dropping it....

Everyone turned up at Croma wearing something pink, everyone had a great time and the cake *was* amazing. We'd booked someone to make balloon animals and the poor woman's fingers were nearly bleeding as she was *hammered* by everyone. Lilly-Mae took it all in her stride with her pink fairy dress – it was the perfect start to Ironman week. We returned home late in the afternoon with Lilly-Mae sparked out for the count. All the attention had taken its toll and she was dead to the world. Once back home and settled, I realised how stressed out I'd been over the little lady's party. A huge weight had been lifted off my shoulders. I know it wasn't a big day in the grand scheme of big days, but I wanted her to have the best birthday she could – even though she had no clue what day it was!

We still had the 'piano' part of the cake and decided to take it with us to Sherborne and have it post race with the other competitors in the B&B. With what seemed like 2,000,000 calories per slice, it would be the perfect snack with a cup of tea the day after the race.

Speaking of which, we had to leave for Ironman the next day......

Chapter 19

Calm before the Storm

The day after Lilly-Mae's birthday was *the* day, or *I-Day* as I termed it – Ironman Day. Amy looked after and organised the little dude whilst I went through my IM checklist a hundred times, packing as I went. Amy had packed her and Lilly-Mae's bag the previous day, all I had to do was sort my stuff out. I was completely paranoid about forgetting something, but then I remembered there would be a huge triathlon expo at the Castle, so if I did forget anything I could buy it if I had to. But given the huge amount of cash I'd already spent, this seemed silly, so just don't forget anything!

With everything checked, re-checked and re-checked again it was time to load the car up. Fitting everything in was going to be a struggle. My bag, Amy's bag, Lilly-Mae's bag, the 'blade, Renny, pushchair and the proverbial kitchen sink – we just managed to squeeze everything in. It was time to set off.

It was a six hour death drive to Sherborne - the motorways were horrendous including the weather. The torrential rain really was a worry. I hoped it would subside for race day. Racing an Ironman in these conditions just wasn't worth contemplating. As we approached the B&B, we had the usual drama of not being able to find it, and when we did we realised we'd driven past it three times, as you do. We unloaded the car and my bikes were put into the garage. I noted the two other bikes already in there. Everyone who was staying at the B&B was there for Ironman. The B&B didn't have a travel cot for Lilly-Mae, despite asking for one. This meant the little lady was in with us – not ideal conditions for a good night's sleep. With everything unpacked, we headed off to get something to eat. It was a thirty minute drive to anywhere decent to eat and I noticed all the signs on the roads informing everyone that the road would be closed on Sunday 20th August. I realised the road we were driving on was part of the bike course so I tried not to pay attention to it, especially the massive hills we seemed to be going up. After finding a great pub and having some decent homemade pub cooking, we headed back to the B&B. Time to try and get a good night's sleep - not easy with a one year old doing tumble turns on you and slapping your shaved head, Benny Hill style.

We got up for breakfast the next day, as opposed to having a lie in, as I wanted to do the swim session in the lake at the castle, which started at 9am. Walking into the breakfast room, two other families were already there, clearly for Ironman. We politely introduced ourselves and exchanged pleasant conversation, whilst managing *not* to actually talk about the impending day of death. We quietly ate breakfast, keeping ourselves to ourselves, apart from Lilly-Mae deciding to play the piano that was in the breakfast room. Grabbing my wetsuit and shower gear, I headed down to the castle. It was a one hour session, plenty of time to familiarise myself with the lake and the layout of the event. The rain still hadn't stopped.

Arriving at the Castle I was surprised at how many people were already there for the swim session. I was also trying to ignore the torrential rain and its implications for race day. Down by the lake, 'Ironman' wetsuits were there, letting people try one of the new Helix suits FOC. For whatever reason, no-one was taking them up on the offer! Why use your own wetsuit when you can trash someone else's? There were no changing facilities, so it was a case of wrapping a towel around yourself whilst getting changed. Which wasn't the case for some Spanish dudes. I turned around and to the most bizarre sight of a hairy arse in my face. It was bizarre because he'd removed his body hair, but not from the top of the thighs upwards, giving him the weird appearance of wearing see through underpants made of body hair. Nice.

Trying to put that out of my mind, I peeled on a Helix medium/large and ventured to the water's edge. A tall, fit looking American woman was in front of me. I didn't realise it at the time, but she was Dede Griesbauer, who would be female champion on race day.

Having raced in the Thames and Salford Quays, I was at least used to water of less than ideal quality, but nothing was going to prepare me for what I can only describe as a massive 'duck toilet'. Not only that, but it was un-seasonably freezing. I eased myself in and began to swim, noting I could only see to my elbow, which was going to make drafting on race day interesting. Try it now – put your arm out in front of you and see where your elbow is. That's how far I could see! I swam to the turnaround point, trying desperately not to swallow any water. My hands and feet were already beginning to get cold on what was just half of the race distance. This was not a good sign. I headed back to the swim start, feeling smug with myself for not filling my own wetsuit with duck shit. Thanks for the loan of the wetsuit 'Ironman'. I made my way to the water's edge, wading through thick green slime to get out. Come back Salford Quays, all is forgiven! I found my kit bag and began peeling the wetsuit off and towelling myself dry. After swimming 2km a shower to get all the duck shit off would have to wait till I got back to the B&B.

I made my way to registration and it was here I got the feeling I was doing a very different race to what I'd done before. It was the *'internationality'* of it. There were all sorts of people from all sorts of countries - America, Spain, Japan, etc. At registration I received my athlete ID card, wristband, swim cap, transition bags and race number '533'. There was no going back now, this was it! I wondered around the tri expo for a while, trying not to buy anything. It was also an opportunity to check the other competitors out. There were some really fit looking people, and some not so fit looking people. It was as mixed a bag of abilities as you'd find at any triathlon, just with different accents. I headed back to the B&B to collect Team Roberts and recce the bike course in the car before lunch.

The bike course was horrendous. Turning out of the Castle you immediately went up a hill, which looked eye bleeding, and it went on like this for 38 miles. My eyes were popping out of my head with each comedy hill that came into site. Amy just laughed manically. There was also a spectacular downhill with an alleged 55mph speed record from the previous year. I made a *'note to self'* to try and at least crack that on the 'blade. Given the heartbreaking nature of the bike course, I sacked off a recce of the run course, deciding that ignorance was bliss. I didn't know it at the time but this was an inspired move. The bike course was also infested with people riding it prior to the race. One question, WHY????? This happened a lot over the next few days, as plenty of people rode the course or could be out seen running prior to race day. IDIOTS! My philosophy was I had plenty of time to get to know the course intimately over the 112 miles. No need to do anymore, besides it was too late now and even the IM training demons were in agreement on that one.

The days leading up to the race plodded by, as did Team Roberts, as I spent them eating as much as possible and buying stuff I didn't need from the triathlon expo in the castle grounds. The 'blade was cleaned, oiled and prepped for the race. It was now, I realised, I'd forgotten my under seat double bottle cage! I panicked and purchased one from the tri expo. Getting it back to the B&B, I went to fit it, but it didn't. The 'blade has a thinner than standard seat post, meaning the bracket was too large. I couldn't believe it. Not only had I forgotten something, despite my meticulous planning, the one I'd just bought didn't fit! What a waste of £40, but it wasn't all bad as Amy claimed it for Babs. The lack of bottle cages could've been a complete disaster. The 'blade only has a single bottle cage so the under seat cages were essential for the long ride. Fortunately for me, aid stations were no more than fifty minutes apart on the three lap bike, so with my aero bottle, one bottle on the bike and maybe one in my cycle jersey, I should be OK. Should be…

Unlike Olympic distance races, for Ironman you pack a red 'run' bag and blue 'bike' bag with everything you need for that discipline and rack them in transition. When you come out of the swim, you run through the blue bag tent, grab the blue bag and get changed, putting your swim stuff in the blue bag. Likewise after the bike leg you run (?) through the red bag tent, grab the red bag and get changed for the run, etc. I'd made the command decision to get changed into fresh kit for each leg of the Ironman. I didn't fancy cycling 112 miles in a wet trisuit with its extremely thin bum pad, then running 26.2 miles in it. I wasn't trying to win the thing! So getting changed into fresh, dry kit seemed like the thing to do. It would mean a few extra minutes in transition, but this was Ironman and taking five extra minutes in transition over a thirteen hour day isn't something to get stressed about. I had to get these bags packed, and in doing so, mistake number 2 reared its head.

I'd done most of my cycling in the Discovery Channel Nike stuff and another set of team branded clothing. Not wanting to do the bike leg in team branded clothing, I'd bought a plain Nike cycle top and plain black Nike bib shorts. I was familiar with the Nike gear, as the Discovery Channel stuff was Nike. Fatal schoolboy error, I hadn't tried them on. When I did put them on at the B&B it was obvious they were completely different to the Discovery Nike gear I was used to. The shoulder straps were twice as thin, meaning they rolled to the width of a piano wire when you had them on. These would cut my shoulders to pieces over 112 miles. Why were they different? Surely Nike medium cycle bib shorts are the same? No, they're not. Also the plain Nike cycle top I got was much larger than the Discovery Channel Nike top, which was supposedly the same size as the one I was used to. Yet another trip to the tri expo in the castle grounds to buy some cycle gear. This could be dangerous in itself as I would be using something I hadn't in training. A quick look around and there was some nice, plain, Ironman branded cycle gear. I felt like I was tempting fate slightly by wearing even more 'Ironman' branded clothing, but it was extremely comfortable with big wide shoulder straps on the bib shorts and plenty of room in the pockets on the cycle top. It also looked fast, which has to be a major consideration when buying any triathlon kit.

With new kit in hand I packed, checked and re-checked everything. It was also time to get the bike ready. The 'blade was practically brand new so didn't require much maintenance. Not that I knew what I was doing anyway. I could oil the chain, but that was it. I packed the bento box with the gels I thought I'd need but not the Danish pastries - I'd buy them last minute and put them in when I arrived in transition race day morning, so they were as fresh as possible. Whilst I was getting the bike ready in the garage of the B&B, two of the other guys came in to do some last minute fiddling. With the bikes that is, not each other.

Dean was Canadian and a multiple Ironman finisher including Hawaii, the other guy was Belgian and I never quite got his name. This was his first Ironman, despite appearing to be over 200 years old. Dean had some great stories and advice, including marking your handlebars with what you've had and when, whether a power gel or bar etc. I didn't really see the point of this at the time. How hard could it be to remember what gels/drinks/bars you'd had when on the bike? I'd find out race day......Dean also told me he'd never done a sub four hour marathon, he made all his time up on the bike. They asked me what gearing I was running – which I clearly had no clue about – I made a mental note to do some sort of bike maintenance course after Ironman. They were both really helpful and it was good to actually talk about race day instead of avoiding it. Everyone was in the same boat, and everyone was as nervous as I was.

With everything packed I dragged it down to transition and racked everything. Learning my lesson from Salford, I covered the 'blade in bin liners to save it from the thunderstorms that kept lashing the place. I saw the Belgian bloke and gave him some bin liners to protect his bike from the inevitable thunderstorm that was going to happen. The race brief was soon after I finished racking everything. Outside the brief tent I bumped into Chris Clarke from Manchester Tri. Chris had already qualified for Hawaii by coming third in his age group in Arizona earlier in the year. He'd also qualified for the 70.3 World Champs in Florida through 70.3 UK by coming top ten overall – wanker. Oh to be that fast……At the race brief we all sat watching the DVD from 2005 World Championships in Hawaii. It was amazing. It truly is the place to get to, and it's understandable why you have to qualify.

The race brief was largely a waste of time and didn't tell me anything I didn't already know from the race information I'd been sent through the post, but it's best to go just in case. In fact they did have one great piece of advice, which was that whilst the roads were technically closed for the race, be aware that some people may still be driving along. With that out of the way, I headed once again back to the B&B to pick Team Roberts up and head to the local town to eat and get some nice pastries for the bike. It was hard to relax, especially knowing that I had to get up at 3.45am the next day. 3.45am was practically still the previous day, wasn't it? The anxiety ramped up as the day progressed. We had a great pub meal in Dorchester, directly on the bike course, where we'd been eating all week. Stuffed, we headed back to the B&B to try and get an early night. I chilled out downstairs in the living room of the B&B, while Amy settled Lilly-Mae. With that done, I tried to get some sleep. This was easier said than done. By trying not to think about race day, that's all I could think about. I'd been training for this for nine months and in a few hours I'd be in the water actually doing it. I just wanted to get going, start the race. Once the start klaxon had sounded, that would be it, nothing would matter from that point, as the race was on! There would be nothing left to worry about, other than finishing, obviously.

Chapter 20

Am I an Ironman?

Just as I managed to get to sleep, my alarm went off. It was 3.45am. I'd actually had six hours sleep, which is pretty good, but it felt like six minutes. I sloped down to breakfast, leaving the girls all snug in bed. We all sat there in near silence, quietly eating porridge. Every second that passed was a second nearer to what was going to be a very very long day. Being so early in the morning meant it was a surreal experience. On the one hand I was faced with what I'd been training all these months for, but on the other hand I just wanted to go back to bed.

With my breakfast of champions eaten, I crept upstairs to grab my white transition bag, which contained everything I needed for after the race - towel, spare clothes, recovery drink, ice packs and tape for the inevitable trashed knees/ankles. Lilly-Mae woke up as I was trying to sneak out of the room and started doing tumble turns on the bed. She gave me a big 'byeeeeeeeeeeee!' whilst flapping her hand. The girls were going to stay at the B&B, as the bike leg went right past it. I'd given them a time window of between 9.15am and 9.45am when I should pass, all being well...

Into the car and through the darkness to the Castle which was packed with 1300 people all about to race. I parked up and slowly walked to transition to make any final adjustments to the 'blade. It was a bizarre scene, all these people milling around transition by floodlight. I found the 'blade and placed the two apple Danish pastries wrapped in foil into the bento box. It was full to capacity, including six painkillers. Walking from the 'blade, I was thinking the next time I'd see it was after the swim. Still in darkness I pulled on my wetsuit and HRM. I packed my white transition bag with the clothes I'd arrived in, along with my 'post race' essentials. Handing the bag over, I looked forward to seeing it again, as the race would be over! All too soon the tannoy called everyone to the swim. Oh shit.......

It was 5.40am and we began pouring into the water. It was 200m to the swim start and the water was FREEZING. The day's first light was just starting to creep across the sky, giving it an eerie glow, as hundreds of people went in. I swam to the left hand side of the start, thinking I was near the back. However, looking over my shoulder to the shore, I could see a seemingly endless swarm of people still getting into the water. I swam around and got warmed up for the Aqua-ruck, preparing myself for the worst. There was no swim brief. We were told at the race briefing the previous day that once everyone was in the water, the only thing we'd hear was the start klaxon. At 6am prompt the klaxon sounded and we were off, to a massive cheer from the crowd that had gathered on the bank.

It wasn't the bun fight I was used to – just busy. There was plenty of pushing and shoving, but nothing like the 'kill or be killed' that I'd experienced in previous races. In Ironman, the swim is all about energy conservation - going crazy to knock three minutes off your swim time is a bit pointless in a 12-15hr day. A puncture on the bike leg will wipe that out twice over. So I was staying calm, staying relaxed and managing to find clear water (as in clear to swim in, not clear to look through). Being able to see only as far as my elbow, a massive 12 inches of visibility ruled drafting out - it would be impossible to see the feet of the person I was drafting, unless I was swimming on top of them. The swim was the thing I was dreading most, when I started the Ironman journey back in November 2005. By the time of that race, it was the least. I knew I could swim the distance and pace myself accordingly. What you can't account for in an event like this, is getting knocked out, which Amy told me had happened to some poor bugger when we met up after the race.

I got to the turnaround point in fifteen minutes. At this pace I was on for a sixty minute swim, way too fast! I eased back, telling myself to relax and conserve energy. The swim was totally uneventful for me, apart from a couple of occasions when I found myself heading way off course. In what seemed no time, I'd done the two laps of the lake and was heading for the swim finish. I kicked my legs like crazy for the last 100m, trying to get some blood into them. Being horizontal for over an hour and mainly using your upper body means there's no blood in the legs. Thrashing them should stop you from falling over when you stand up, but I still fell over as soon as I stood up out of the water, as the blood rushed away from my head. Getting back up I instinctively ran the 100m to the bag tent, as if in an OD race, still trying to get blood and heat into my legs, with the crowd cheering wildly for everyone. I'd done the swim in 1.09, which wasn't a PB, but I was fresh and that time was in a crowd of 1300 people. Through the blue bag tent and I grabbed bag '533'. Time to get cycling for the next six hours or so....

As I'd opted to get changed into full cycling gear rather than tackle the 112 miles in a wet tri suit, I spent a little extra time in T1. But it was worth it to be in dry kit that I knew would be comfortable for the ride. I towelled myself dry and tried to get the cycling bib shorts on over my damp skin, which was almost impossible - your skin needs to be bone dry, not damp. I wasted precious time fighting the bib shorts as they refused to go over my legs and torso. I eventually got them on, feeling almost as tired as from doing the swim! I had a tub of Vaseline in each transition bag. I'd learned from the long training rides you need a good lubing with the stuff between your thighs – which I unceremonially did in front of everyone.

With cycling gear on, I chucked all my swim gear into the bag and handed it to the race crew as I ran out to collect the 'blade. T1 time 8 mins – which sounds bad, but that's from getting out of the water, running 100m to transition, getting dried, changed, running the 100m to get my bike and out across the timing mat. I'd come out of the water with 570th fastest time (or slowest in my case) place and managed to set the 887th slowest time in T1!

I knew what was coming on the bike leg, so cycling out of the castle past the cheering crowd was fine, but I knew it was straight into the first of many, many, many hills. I was straight into my smallest gear (which I've never used before) and again kept telling myself not to go mad on the adrenalin rush you get from all the crowd cheering and the general elation of finishing the swim. At the top of the first hill a crowd had already gathered and was cheering us on. I was telling myself to enjoy the race and enjoy the crowd, which might sound crazy but you only get to do your first Ironman once, so you may as well try to enjoy it.

Over the top and into some nice rolling downhills through picture postcard villages, and someone was by the side of the road fixing a puncture already. This was something I didn't want to think about, having to stop and fix a puncture, but in that first thirty minutes I saw at least four people doing it. The 'blade didn't have the puncture resistant tyres like Renny, but Mike at Bridgtown Cycles found me some tyres that offered puncture resistance, whilst not compromising rolling resistance. As to what they were, check 'Kenda' tyres out. Did they work? No puncture at all during Ironman.

Pedalling along the roads it was time to get *'the plan'* into action. *'The plan'* was my race and nutrition plan - what to eat, plus what HR limits to stay in, and when. For the first hour I stuck to the bananas I'd grabbed on my way out of the swim, as I didn't want to start on gels too soon, I had plenty of time to get sick of those later on. After the first hour I'd have a gel every 30-45 minutes, one bottle of water every hour and one bottle of energy drink every hour, keeping my HR below 150bpm. Me and the 'blade were spinning along nicely and had tackled the first set of hills OK. There was a great crowd at the top of one hill, with *'Tour de France'* type messages scrawled in the road. The crowd gave a massive cheer as a girl caught and overtook me at the top – all credit to her. What they didn't see was her slow to a crawl with a purple face 200m further on, with the grim realisation we had another 90 miles to go sinking in. Ironman is no place for heroics - I'd learnt that lesson with the swim nemesis.

At the turnaround point was the pub where we'd been eating all week and where things started to go wrong. When approaching an aid station you need to slow down, and not to 20mph from 30mph. Trying to snatch bottles at 20mph simply resulted in them bouncing out of my hand and all over the road. I had to tackle the next ten miles on water and power gels at a point where the hills became obscene. It was now one hour of solid climbing. Again it was down into bottom gear and trying to blank out the fact I had to do this three times. People were already walking up one particular hill called 'The Giant', an undulating monster that stretched uphill as far as you could see. It was at this point I realised I was doing an Ironman. Oh dear, oh dear. The only good thing was looking forward to the 14% hill the other side.

Once at the top I smashed into top gear and went for the 55mph record down the hill. The 'blade loved it. I rocketed down, 40mph, 45mph, 50mph, 52mph, 53.5mph then ran out of road. Oh well, I clocked one of the fastest times of the day but not the 55mph record. Someone did crack 55mph, swiftly followed by their collarbone and bike as they hit a water bottle and ended up in a field. Not pretty.

I also had to stop for a pee, which is easier said than done when wearing cycle bib shorts or even a trisuit. I'd been dying for a piss for most of the first lap and didn't want to stop, but you have to give in to nature at some point. At least I didn't need to wreak anal devastation! I ended up stopping twice per lap in almost the same place every time. At least I knew I was hydrating properly. I considered simply pissing myself, as some people do, standing up in the peddles and letting the golden flow go. I suppose it saves time, but do you really want to cycle 112 miles in piss soaked pants?

Back on the bike and back to the reality of grinding away. After 1hr 50mins I came up towards the B&B where Amy was stood with Lilly-Mae. It was great to see them and I was more or less on time. They gave me a big cheer and with that I knew the first lap was almost complete. This kept the morale topped up, as I went onto the first lap completion point and I'd somehow managed to set the 400th fastest time - in the top 3rd for the first lap – but could I keep it up? I couldn't. Back to the rolling hills through the villages, making way for two ambulances as I did so – someone's IM had ended in tears. The hill with the crowd on top beckoned again. The first time it had been horrendous, second time it was heartbreaking. Everyone was staring blankly at the road three feet beyond the front wheel. I was trying to ignore the burning in my legs. It was tough shit.

Rolling back through the villages and a car appeared from nowhere, driving at 60mph! I looked on in disbelief. OK, so maybe someone had to get somewhere but this car was clearly being driven by a 'NIMBY' (Not In My Back Yard), driving at full tilt, knowing full well 1300 cyclists were on the road. This got worse as the laps went on, to the point where I wondered if they'd actually re-opened the roads. There were plenty of locals out in the driveways of the cottages spurring us on with much needed encouragement, but there were equally as many who clearly didn't give a shit, all of them seemingly over 50, driving Volvo estates , with a penchant for tweed.

The rest of the lap degenerated into nothing but misery and as the 60 mile point approached, I began to crumble both physically and mentally, just like my first long ride. The *'Giant'* came round again and this time there were even more people walking with their bikes. People were walking, crying and fixing punctures. Every bit of bike accessory you can think of was lying by the road at some point. By now I'd lost track of what gels I'd had and when I'd had them. Dean and his tip of marking what you've had on your handlebars suddenly made perfect sense. My plan was coming apart at the seams. I didn't think it would be difficult to keep track of things, but you're trying so hard you do lose track of what you've had and when. Did I grab one gel or two at the last feed station? Am I *on* my fifth gel or have I already *had* my fifth gel? I hadn't factored in the energy drink to any of the plan, other than to try and have at least one bottle per hour. These were extra calories on top of those in the plan and this turned out to be an inspired move, as the difference in concentration of the drink between feed stations was huge. Some were exactly as if I'd made them myself but others tasted like water that had some powder spilt in them by accident. The only thing keeping me going was the knowledge that to stop would spell disaster and simply prolong the pain.

My back was in agony, I'd developed a sharp stabbing pain in my left ankle, my shoulders were locked and my knees had aged 100 years. The only thing I had to look forward to was gagging down yet another of the seemingly three million gels I'd already had that day. But wait?! Didn't I have some Danish's?!? Oh yes! At the top of *The Giant* I treated myself to half a Danish - it was sweet, sweet nectar, something savoury! This did the trick of perking me up - having something savoury was such a nice change to the sickly sweet gels – it was heaven. Towards the end of the second lap I was passing Team Roberts outside the B&B, with a much needed cheer to spur me on. A few miles further down the road and at the lap completion T-Junction I turned left onto – THE LAST LAP.

As I peddled along, a strange noise was nagging me. There was a tonne of vibration from the road which the 'blade's carbon frame was doing a great job of absorbing. But these are still crap British roads with speed sapping road surfaces, so maybe it was just road vibration. I kept glancing down, but nothing seemed to be wrong. Grabbing my bottle out of the cage, I knew what was wrong immediately, the bottle cage had vibrated loose and was attached by just a few millimetres of thread. This could be a huge disaster - if the cage fell off with a bottle in, and went into my wheel, it could have me off in a big way. I screeched to a stop and grabbed the allen keys out of my tool bag under the seat... except they weren't there! Then it struck me like a tax bill from the inland revenue - I'd left them in Lilly-Mae's bedroom along with the underseat bottle cage. This *was* a disaster. what was I going to do? I hand tightened the bolts as best I could and set off at full tilt, but it was just a matter of minutes before they vibrated loose again.

I could see a policeman at one of the major junctions with someone who had already called it a day on the bike. I screeched to a halt, breathlessly asking if any of them had allen keys. The copper didn't and the girl who'd binned it didn't either. I hand tightened the bolts again, hammered off and within minutes the bolts had come loose again. This created huge anxiety. What should I do? The answer presented itself at the next aid station - an ambulance with a bike propped up against it. Clearly the rider was inside. It was a decent looking bike, and more importantly, it had a tool kit under the seat. I stopped, and without hesitating, opened the tool kit, looking for an allen key to fit my bottle cage. There was a comprehensive bike tool inside with a key to fit my bolts, which I tightened to a point where I thought it might crack the carbon frame if I went any further. I replaced the tool, jumped back on the 'blade and set off again. It might not have been a puncture, but I'd had to stop three times. I cursed my schoolboy error. But to whoever was in that ambulance, cheers for the loan of your bike tool.

The third lap was bizarre, I struggled through to the 80 mile point, then entered some kind of bizarre feeling of euphoria. I couldn't work out whether this was:

A) due to too many power gels
or
B) not enough power gel

Whatever the reason I felt really good. Actually I knew I didn't 'feel' good but was simply in some sort of manic state of happiness. Maybe this is what Japanese kamikaze pilots felt like just before they dive bombed to their deaths? Was it so soul destroying? Had I gone over the edge into the strange place of feeling great? I'd been through the 'paranoia' stage earlier in the lap, convinced my tyres were going flat, I was being drafted, I'd been penalised for drafting when I hadn't been, etc. At one aid station a guy was standing there talking to himself and walking round in circles, with the race crew trying to talk to him. I couldn't end up like that, I had to keep going.

Just before the next aid station some enterprising local kids had set up their own 'bottle drop'. Just before a station you chuck your empties into a taped off area. These kids had set one up 50m before the real one. I didn't realise till I'd gone past and it brought a smile to my face. They had a massive pile already and I can't imagine how many they would've collected during the day or how they got them all home. It was a brief moment of amusement that took my mind off things for a few seconds.

Rather than question this general feeling of euphoria, I pressed on as a six hour bike was on the cards. I even had the energy to acknowledge everyone that cheered for the last 15 miles. Team Roberts wasn't outside the B&B, as they had moved down to transition, but this was great as I knew I was less than three miles from getting off the bike. 109 miles gone and seven hours something total time showing on the HRM. The last two miles to the Castle were downhill, which was such a massive relief, and I was still riding the wave of this bizarre euphoria.

Into the Castle grounds and the huge crowd was going nuts for everyone. It really did lift me and keep me going. I jumped off the bike and the feel good factor just got better – off the bike at last. One of the race crew took my bike for me and I jogged through to the red bag tent to grab my run gear. I peeled the cycling gear off, towelled down, whacked Vaseline under my arms, on my nipples, etc, pulled the running gear on, and out of transition with 8hrs showing on the HRM. It was 2pm. I'd been working continually since 6am and up since 3.45am. All I had to do now was run a marathon, which I'd never run before. I'd decked a couple of pain killers on the last mile of the bike, figuring the feel good factor would soon come to an end. It would.

I set off at a 9 minute mile pace, just sneaking the possibility of a 4hr marathon. I finished the bike with the 805th slowest time and left T2 in 689th slowest time after taking six minutes to get in and out. My original goal was to finish the event, then maybe under fifteen hours or even, best case scenario, in the twelve hour bracket. But a lot can happen in 26 miles and the sharp, stabbing pain in my ankle had returned. It was great to be off the bike though, standing upright and moving my legs in a different way. I didn't experience the jelly leg syndrome, but given the ragged state of mind and body, that's not surprising.

The run was an unknown for two reasons:

1) I hadn't recce'd it
2) I'd never ran a marathon before

I knew we had two laps to complete around the castle grounds and as per everything to do with IMUK, it was very hilly. But this didn't bother me, I was still in my strange mental place and still enjoying *not* being on the bike. The two laps around the castle grounds were great, and coming back through transition the crowd gave you the lift you needed. I even started to allow myself to think I was going to finish, and in the twelve hour bracket. I was sticking to my plan of walking the aid stations and taking a bit of everything on offer apart from the coco-cola and power gels, and running in between.

After coming through transition to start the second lap of the castle grounds, I saw Amy and Lilly-Mae! They gave me a big cheer, which gave me the lift I needed at just the right time. After six miles of running I still felt OK and was still in the 9 minute mile bracket. Approaching one of the many large hills in the grounds, plenty of people were walking, including an American lady. I passed her and didn't think anything of it. However, two miles later, I passed her again?! Sadly ,people do cheat at Ironman and I was shocked that someone would do so. What's the point?

Back through transition again and this time the run route

took us through the town and up to the ten mile point. At this pace I was still on for a four hour marathon and possibly, just possibly, a sub twelve hour Ironman. From this point on I was in unknown territory as I hadn't recce'd the run route, and things went downhill, rapidly.

The feel good factor evaporated as we peeled onto a dual carriageway. I didn't know it at the time, but I had fifteen miles of this. I was to name it the 'Road of the Damned'. Running along, I could see two sets of mile markers, one which was clearly relevant to me and another which was obviously meant for a second lap. I went into paranoid mode again, convinced it was wrong, then became enraged with myself for not recce'ing the run route. As I dragged myself along the featureless road, I started hating everybody and everything. Whose idea was it to run along a dual carriageway for fifteen miles? IDIOTS! AAAAAAAAAARGH!

I was now slowly sinking into the depths of a dark place, realising I did indeed have fifteen miles of this. Just as I came to that realisation, I crested the brow of a small hill, to be confronted with something that stretched into the distance for 1½ miles in front of me. I called it 'Hamburger Hill'. This is where things went even more downhill than they already were, or uphill to be more exact. I didn't mind the hills so much, but doing them on the dual carriageway really pissed me off. It showed a total lack of imagination on the organiser's part, or the local council, and I certainly wouldn't fancy my chances on the Road of the Damned if I was one of the backmarkers running in the night, with nothing but a day-glo stick and line of tape to stop someone from mowing me down. All the beautiful Dorset countryside around us, but we get to stare at a dual carriageway for 15 miles.

By now I wasn't sure what was happening and was moving on instinct, convinced if I stopped to walk I'd be talking to myself and dribbling at an aid station. The aid stations themselves became a blur of power gels, water and pretzels (for the salt). I'd be going for ten hours with nothing for company but my own thoughts and, as I suspected, this is where Ironman really gripped me – the mental game. Looking at people as I passed them and as they passed me, going in the other direction, everyone looked to be in a personal space of torture, both physically and mentally - a bit like *'The Arndale Centre'* in Manchester. You end up passing and be passed by the same people. As they walk you pass them, as you go through an aid station they pass you. I did this with one particular guy for half an hour - every time he trotted passed me I knew I'd pass him again further along the road as he stopped to dry heave.

Up and over *Hamburger Hill* to be confronted by, oh yes, another hill. Eventually I got to the turnaround point, which was fifteen miles in total for me. It was manned by some squaddies who'd rigged up some 'M*A*S*H style tents in a lay-by, with some non-descript music blaring out. The timing mat was also here. I started playing the *'next-time-I'm-here-only-five-miles-to-go game'*. But obviously I had the small matter of another seven miles to do before that, including *Hamburger Hill* again.

The Road of the Damned did have some spectators on it cheering you on. They had competitor lists and would look your name up as you approached, shouting *'come on Darren!'* This actually brought a lump to my throat... which signified I'd reached rock bottom emotionally. Instead of crumbling any further under the pain, I had to dig myself out of this hole. Ironman is meant to be a journey, and some people 'share' that journey with each other by clinging together in small groups on the run to get each other through it. I'm not into using psychological crutches or being used as one, so I hadn't even looked at anyone else, let alone speak to them. I now began to pay attention to my fellow competitors, almost using their suffering to help me along. There's always someone worse off than you, right? On the *Road of the Damned* they weren't in short supply.

Entering one aid station, a guy simply collapsed onto the floor in a heap. He held his head in his hands and I'm sure he was sobbing. Rather you than me, mate, I thought. He was extremely fit looking, but coach Kiddle told me that the people who you'd think will do well, actually die, whilst random looking people plod by, nice as you like. Another guy was berating himself for being *'...so fucking stupid!... this is fucking shit!... mumble mumble...'.* Indeed - a moment of clarity we could have all done with having before entering Ironman.

At the end of the dual carriageway again, another turnaround point and the heartbreaking act of having to go back onto the *Road of the Damned,* as opposed to the two miles to the finish. The aid station at this point was full of people talking themselves out of finishing. I'd made up over 300 places by this point, after leaving T1, and this was the ultimate final grind. It took a Herculean effort to go back out onto the *Road of the Damned*, but what was the other option? Sit down at the aid station talking to myself and throw away all the months of hard work and sacrifice? It's called *'Ironman'* for a reason, not *'slightly-difficult-man'* or *'might-be-a-bit-tough-on-the-day-man'*. I'd slowed to 9½ - 10 minute mile pace by this stage, making a four hour marathon impossible, but finishing in the 12 hour bracket was still on the cards.

Back out onto the *Road of the Damned*, all I had to do was five or six miles, then I'd be back here again, and instead of going back out onto the hell road, I could blast the two miles to the finish. My target was to catch the person in front and not let anyone past, and this I did. The amount of people walking was amazing, I never stopped jogging. Not because I was super fit and tough but I simply didn't want to drag it out any longer and walking would do just that. I had to switch off mentally, apart from to look at the tortured faces of those coming in the other direction to make myself feel better. Not in the spirit of Ironman, but this was a matter of survival, so anything went as far as I was concerned.

Over *Hamburger Hill* and at last I could see the Army manned M*A*S*H post with the pumping music, only there weren't any hot nurses scantily dressed, which surely would have helped. Over the timing mat and the last five miles of the marathon started here, five simple miles. I had two painkillers left in my tiny zip pocket on my running shorts and I decked them to take the edge off. On that last final stretch I looked at everyone coming the other way, knowing this was it for me. The look of pain on their faces and imagining them having to do another lap - did I keep feeding off them to boost myself or did I offer words of encouragement? I upped the pace slightly at this point and knew I could get a 4½ hour marathon. With just four miles to go now I could afford to be a bit cavalier with the energy consumption.

At the end of the *Road of the Damned* and the final aid station. Except this time I could carry on to the finish just two miles away, as all the poor bastards behind me had to go back onto the *Road of the Damned*. I really upped the pace now, breaking into 8 minute miles on legs that were so far gone it didn't matter anymore, as I knew I was going to finish somewhere near 12½ hours, which was my best case scenario. It felt like I was sprinting, but in reality it was no more than a slow run.

Through the town and coming the other way were a string of people who hadn't even started on the *Road of the Damned* yet. I tried not to catch their eyes in case they cheered me on and I blurted out what was in store for them. I felt like I was looking at people about to go over the top of the trenches in WWI - they were doomed. One mile to go. Half a mile to go. The crowds on the side of the road were going mad, the race crew were shouting at you. Into the castle grounds and up the finishing chute. The crowd was great. I was high fiving all the kids as I ran down, soaking up the atmosphere. You only get to do this for the *first time* once, and I was determined to enjoy it.

I was looking for Amy and Lilly-Mae, as I wanted to run through the finish line with the little dude. I couldn't see them and as I ran down across the finish line with everyone cheering, the race announcer called my name as I crossed the line, the iconic Ironman finish under the big clock with arms raised. Someone placed a finisher medal around my neck. I'd done it, I was an Ironman. I was fucked.

I could see the girls directly in front of me. I felt strangely good. I'd felt much worse physically after a hard training session, but this was all pure adrenalin. The sense of achievement was intoxicating. I couldn't believe I'd actually done it, I'd played it out in my head so many times and now I was actually experiencing it. I had to go and get changed and sort myself out. The race crew took my timing chip off for me. I ambled to the barriers to kiss Amy and get a hug from the little dude, as well as the obligatory photo.

Ironman UK 2006 – Practising my finish, I wasn't far wrong...

Ironman UK 2006 – The 'blade, fully loaded.

Ironman UK 2006 – 12 miles on the bike done, just another 100 miles to go.....

Ironman UK 2006 – 6 miles down, just 20.2 to go and the '*Road of the Damned*', twice...

Ironman UK 2006 – I'd done it, it was over, I was an Ironman.

I was then ushered into the athlete recovery area by the race crew. Friends and family weren't allowed in this part, which was a shame because I didn't know what I was doing – all my energy was being used for gross motor control like walking and breathing, I didn't have anything left for decision making. I wandered around in circles for a bit before collecting my white transition bag. I hadn't seen this bag since 5.30am where I'd thought to myself *'next time I see this I'm finished'*, and here I was.

I found a chair and sat down, realising at this point that my legs had completely seized and I wasn't sure I'd be able to stand up again. The queue for the massage tent was massive and at least 50m away. Which may as well have been fifty miles as far as I was concerned. Simply trying to decide whether to go for it or not was like trying to work out some quantum physics equation. I started to get changed, then noticed the huge hot tubs! I had to get some hot tub action, that would sort me right out. I headed for the hot tubs via the food tent which was full of savoury snacks, pork pies, sausage rolls, soup etc This may sound bizarre but that's exactly what you're craving. Unfortunately my stomach had shrunk to the size of a pea, so I couldn't eat as much as I wanted. Having stuffed a few sausage rolls into my mouth, I headed to the nearest hot tub and got in. Everyone was going through their Ironman story but I was too far gone for conversation. It was funny, sat there listening to everyone tell their Ironman tale, fuelled by a cocktail of testosterone and the sense of relief it was really over. One guy actually couldn't stop talking and his jaw was making some strange movements. The more he talked the more something wasn't right. Where was he getting his energy from? Then the answer came in his description of his race nutrition plan, which involved massive amounts of pro-plus caffeine tablets. Had I not been so exhausted, I would've laughed out loud, but could only manage a smirk. This guy may have been feeling OK now, but the huge amount of caffeine he'd had was going to massively cock up his recovery process! He was going to feel ten times worse than he should!

With that I peeled myself out of the hot tub, and immediately went into an uncontrollable shaking fit. It was so bad I couldn't pick my towel up or get changed out of my wet shorts. I forced myself to keep moving and was able to get my dry kit on, still shaking like a leaf. Once dressed I looked at my recovery drink. The thought of having another sport-type drink nearly made me throw up so I binned it, but did manage to force down an electrolyte drink.

Once the shakes were under control, I ventured back out to where the girls were waiting. It was time to get out of dodge. I handed my white transition bag to Amy and hobbled off to transition to collect my bags and the 'blade. This was a task in itself, as I couldn't actually walk properly. I walked very, very slowly through transition collecting my red and blue bags, before retrieving the 'blade from its position on the rack. I headed out, having my athlete wristband cut off as I left. Once you had all your gear, you weren't allowed back in. This was all a bit bizarre as it followed the exact same protocol as any other triathlon. I asked myself if I'd just done an Ironman? It wasn't an anti climax or anything like that, just a bit strange. I hobbled out of transition. My legs were absolutely crippled. The girls were waiting for me by the car park and we made our way to the car. A steady stream of people were finishing, and some people were just heading out on the run! The waves of relief started to wash over me again. It was over. All I had to do now was to try and get in the car......

Amy drove back to the B&B after I'd eventually got myself

into the car. I wasn't looking forward to getting out of it. What I was looking forward to was a steaming hot bath as soon as we got into the room. We arrived at the B&B and I began the long journey from the car up the stairs. I was walking like someone the age of Kiddle. It took me ten minutes to get to the room, where I put the bath on immediately. Sitting on the bed waiting for the bath to fill up, Lilly-Mae jumped on my legs. It was excruciating. The best way to describe the feeling is that of being horrendously bruised from top to bottom. The other thing I realised was that this pain was probably masking other problems with my shoulders, feet, etc.

Whatever was going on, all I could think about was a bath, and a massive meal, the fattier the better. With the bath run, I eased myself into it, whilst Amy sorted all my gear out, bless her. The bath was perfect, but it did nothing to ease the pain. I taped an ice pack to my ankle, which had been bothering me during the race. It wasn't hurting now but my arms could've been on fire and it's doubtful I would've noticed.

We headed out to Dorchester to our usual pub, which also did an impressive apple pie and custard that had my name all over it. I was drooling in the car thinking about it. Amy asked if I could eat another PowerGel for my life. I nearly threw up everywhere and told her it would be curtains for me. We got to the pub and ordered our meal. My eyes were like saucers as I ordered way too much food. It was the full Sunday lunch for me with an ice cold lager shandy! When the food arrived I started to attack it, but having survived on nothing but gels for twelve hours, my pea sized stomach couldn't take it. I tried to eat as much as I could but ended up leaving half of it – gutted. I still ate the apple pie and custard though, even if it meant exploding, Mr Creosote style, as in Monty Python's 'Meaning of Life'.

It was 9pm when we eventually left the pub and it was just starting to get dark. I pointed out to Amy that people would still be out on the *Road of the Damned*, alone and with a glo-stick stuck to their backs for safety. I was more than happy to be finished, bathed and fed. It's an Ironman tradition that you go back to the finish line and cheer the last finishers across before the cut off at 11pm. As bad as this sounds, frankly I didn't care. All I wanted to do was get back to the B&B and get some rest, not spend more time on my feet. We got back to the B&B and I made the long journey up the short steps, I eased myself onto the bed and tried to relax. Unfortunately, the throbbing in my legs was so bad I didn't get any sleep. Every time I tried to move, the pain would wake me up. It was muscle soreness of the most extreme order!

After a terrible night's sleep, I headed down to breakfast. In the room, everyone else was sat there. Unlike that first morning where we talked about everything *but* Ironman, here the only topic of conversation was Ironman, how wrecked you were and any interesting race stories. Dean had finished in 10½ hours. Some random American dude, who we hadn't seen all week but was there at breakfast, had just managed to get in before the cut off, and me at 12½ hours, all walking as if we had wooden legs. It doesn't matter what time you finish Ironman in, the point is you finish. I'd set myself a goal of finishing in a certain time and had been lucky enough to do it.

We were all going to the ceremony held in the castle grounds at lunchtime, where the top three males and top three females were to get their awards, followed by the top three in each age group, who would also qualify for Hawaii. With everything packed onto the car, we headed down to the Castle, but once inside I couldn't be arsed with it. We had a huge drive ahead of us. It had seemed like a good idea at the time to attend the ceremony, but once there, it seemed pointless. So we squeezed out the back door and started the long journey home.

Chapter 21

Ironman, the aftermath....

Getting back to Manchester and for once I didn't go straight online to pour over the results. Who gave a shit? I'd finished, that was enough. There also weren't any '*what if*' scenarios, I couldn't have done it any differently given the training I'd done for it. It went as well as it possibly could've done, which was another satisfying factor. I was supposed to carry on training lightly in the week following Ironman, but my ankle was extremely painful, so I'd booked myself in to see my physio as soon as we got back home. Kiddle said it was imperative I continue to train lightly in the post Ironman week, which I already knew as it aids the recovery process. But with a crocked ankle it wasn't on the cards, and my knees felt like they were made out of soft cheese.

I spent the time texting everyone telling them I was an Ironman - another extremely satisfying thing! I told Jason and Darren they may have Olympic gold's but I had an Ironman finisher's medal. I told Lee she may have

Commonwealth bronze but I had an Ironman finisher's medal, etc, etc. You get the picture. I was still basking in the glory of my sense of achievement, which hadn't worn off, despite being the next day. In fact it wouldn't wear off for a good week, about the same time as my legs took to get back to normal. The DOMS, (Delayed Onset of Muscle Soreness - although there was nothing 'delayed' about it, as they began to hurt as soon as I stopped), was made worse by not being able to train lightly to speed the recovery up. Playing with Lilly-Mae was a beasting, as she loved to climb all over my legs whilst I was sat on the living room floor, which was bloody painful!

I spent a lot of time recounting my story to everyone and how horrendous it was, as well as writing my post race report for everyone in my e-mail address book. I'd even managed to raise £1000 for the Rainbow Trust, so the reports were just a way of letting everyone who'd sponsored me know how I was getting on in the build up to Ironman. Now I could tell them how I'd done it and more importantly – I'd finished.

The next best thing about finishing an Ironman after the sense of achievement is the holiday you deserve with the family. There has to be a pay off for your triathlon admin support team (family) for all the standing around they've done all season, all the hours you've spent with your bike and in the pool, as opposed to with them. In our case this was a month long trip to Southern California, to our favourite stomping ground Laguna Beach. I'd booked the trip and rented the cottage back in June, and managed to keep it a secret from our friends in California, who we were going to surprise by simply knocking on their door when we arrived. Unfortunately at the end of my Ironman race report I announced we were going to California where I was going to put my 13kgs back on, letting the cat out of the bag. So ten days after Ironman, Team Roberts departed for an extremely well earned rest in sunnier climes.

It was the perfect place to go, right on the Ocean on Pacific Coast Highway – a small beach place called the *'White Picket Fence'* cottage. The flight was horrendous, obviously. As I've said before, flying is officially the most inconvenient way to travel, unless you have your own jet of course. But none of this mattered, like driving in rush hour down the 405 Freeway from Los Angeles to Laguna taking 1½ hours instead of forty five minutes. It didn't matter because it was 80° in September, I had NO TRAINING to do whatsoever or work for the next month and it was family time all the way.

Arriving in Laguna we settled into the post-card cottage overlooking the ocean, chilling out on the balcony with an ice cold Corona (I couldn't remember the last time I had a beer)...and being an Ironman. I now had plenty of time to reflect on what I'd done and what meaning, if any, there was to it. I knew why I'd done it, I knew why I got into it – but did it give me anything? I was no stranger to testing myself, I'd been in some extremely testing situations in the military and had pushed myself beyond my physical abilities before. But that was years ago, and to be in that place again where it's you against yourself was something I'd forgotten.

During the race I'd used everyone else's suffering to spur me along, which isn't really in the spirit of Ironman. But I'd done all the six hour rides, two hour swims and three hour runs on my own, so the last thing I wanted to do was start clinging to people to help each other get through it. I also had this irrational fear that if I did start helping someone along, then my mojo would start disappearing through some bizarre osmosis. I'm not saying that you shouldn't work together with someone on the bike or run during an Ironman, I just wanted to test myself to breaking point with no help from anyone but myself.

But that still left the questions as to why I'd chosen to go it alone? Was it simply because I'd trained on my own? And why had I trained on my own anyway? I knew Nick and Chris at Manchester tri, surely I could've crashed some sessions with them or with someone from the club? There were at least two other girls doing Ironman UK from Manchester Tri. Ironman is a journey of self discovery, not just a physical test to the limit. As I've mentioned before, you spend a long time on your own, and it breaks you down to what you really are – which in my case is slightly selfish.

Let me explain that. Maybe 'selfish' is the wrong word – I don't sit watching the wife carry heavy shopping bags into the house whilst I drink a Stella in my stained white vest asking where my dinner is. I've stopped on two occasions to help people that were having epileptic fits and administered first aid without thinking, as I was trained to do by the forces. Driving to the last race of the 2006 BSB season at Brands Hatch, it was getting dark and had just started raining when I drove past a car on the hard shoulder of the M25 with it's hazards on. I noticed it was a young woman with a kid around the same age as my daughter. So I drove to the next junction, turned round and drove all the way back to the junction past the woman, to turn back round again just to stop and check she was OK. I then called the Surrey Police to make sure they'd picked her up on the motorway CCTV and someone was on the way. I'd done it because it was the right thing to do and I hoped someone would do the same for Amy, who hopefully wasn't an axe murderer. So maybe selfish is the wrong word.

It's all to do with being a squaddie and the way we're trained. We're not trained to be selfish, in fact the exact opposite. You live in each other's pockets when on operational tour and have to trust each other with your lives, but if you're not 'one of us' and are capable of looking after yourself then you're not considered. I've carried this on in civvie street. My 'team' is my immediate family and close friends. No one else registers on the radar. People who meet me for the first time can think I'm either ignorant or arrogant. I'm neither. I'm just not into going out of my way to make people like me or create a good impression – you're not in 'my team'. But once in 'my team' I'll do anything for you, as it was in the forces. But to be part of the 'team' takes more than a couple of handshake introductions through mutual friends, you have to put the time in! This is part of the reason I've been successful in sport, it's a very similar working environment to the forces, all boys together and all that.

I also thought back to my 2002 triathlon club experience and how much the cold shoulder treatment from the other guys was as much to do with me. The answer obviously is that it was as much to do with me as them. Yeah, they were totally unfriendly, but being my belligerent self can't have endeared them to me either.

So when it came to training for Ironman and racing one, I simply reverted to base instinct – concentrate on my 'team', which for the purposes of Ironman, consisted of me. So the reality was I was doing what I knew best, working with my team and working well, even though it was just me. When it came to race day I wasn't interested in helping or being helped by anyone. We'd all entered Ironman, we knew what we were getting into and we'd all trained for it to a greater or lesser degree. So come race day and it all starts going wrong, unless it's through injury it's no-one's fault but your own. It never even occurred to me to train with someone or help someone on race day, it simply wasn't in my makeup.

I'm not saying this is right or wrong, but what was actually driving me through all of this. I knew why I'd entered Ironman, now I was working out what got me through and why I'd done it that way. If I had have worked with someone during the race then there's every possibility I would've finished in a quicker time. Then again they could've slowed me down. Had I trained with someone then it would've all been a damn sight easier to get through the training sessions, but would that have prepared me mentally for race day?

If you've got any personal demons or skeletons in the closet, I think these could come back to haunt you during an Ironman so you'd better be prepared to face them down. The only reason I say this is because all I had to focus my mental energy on was keeping myself going, not by having to rationalise events or decisions that I'd made in my life during the twelve hours of the race. It may seem that all you do have to think about during Ironman is finishing. Trust me, over the six to eight hours you could take on the bike and the four to six hours you could take on the run, you've got plenty of time to explore your own mind.

For me this is why most people fail, they succumb to the mental demands of Ironman. Over 150 people didn't finish Ironman UK, which out of 1300 who entered isn't that bad.

But of those 150 how many pulled out early because they'd had enough and not through injury? As I've mentioned before, the aid stations on the bike and run are full of people standing around talking themselves out if finishing. With no-one and nothing to motivate them but themselves, they suddenly discover they don't have the mental strength to finish. I'm not saying that if you enter an Ironman and don't finish you're going to spend the next six months sat in a dark room wearing nothing but coffee stained underpants mumbling to yourself, but remember it's called 'Ironman' for a reason. I can't emphasise the mental aspect of Ironman enough and I know I'm harping on a bit, but the demons I faced down in terms of training for it and maintaining a sense of reality paled in comparison to the mental effort of race day.

The other thing to consider was the training lessons I'd learned and the practical knowledge I'd gained. Despite what I've said, Kiddle's training programmes did have a logical progression and periodisation. However, with missing so many sessions every month, when it came to the next training month I had to tell Kiddle what I'd managed to do and based on that he would knock another programme up. After nine months of training and the programmes that go with it I'm fairly confident I can self train, but I've no doubt that I'll be on the phone to Kiddle for some direction at some point, it's inevitable. I'd also assumed, wrongly, that my vocational training would give me a massive advantage when it came to the practical side of the training for Ironman. As I've said before though, it doesn't matter what you know or don't know – Ironman is so far removed from anything, it's a great leveller. The only advantage in training I could see from my job was the 'test as you train', policy which I've already discussed.

The one unforeseen benefit was the respect from athletes in the other sports I work in. 12½ hours isn't going to bother anyone's place on the GB long distance team in my age group by a long stretch, obviously. But given my previous size and level of endurance fitness (none) everyone was impressed and thought I was insane in equal measure. Meeting new athletes as part of my job, the conversation would inevitably turn to the training I did myself, where I would say I was just getting into triathlon and completing Ironman distance. This would always bring a low whistle from the athlete along with a shake of the head. I had no problem taking any compliments about it, and neither should anyone who has finished an IM. It's a collosal achievement and you should revel in it for as long as possible, regardless of your finish time. Remember – a finish is a finish.

The rest of the trip to the US was spent mainly eating, and if you want to eat then the best place in the world to be is in the US! With portions amounting to almost treble what you'd get in the UK I was attacking the 13kg weight loss deficit aggressively. I couldn't not train at all, so I ran every other day and did a weight session every other day with Tim (our friends who live there). But with the runs being only thirty minutes and having not done weights all year, it was all straight forward and not the life consuming sessions I'd had to do for Ironman. I also ran with Amy pushing Lilly-Mae in the trolley, which Lilly-Mae loved! She'd hold her arms up as if on a rollercoaster and laugh the whole way. Running as a family isn't something we can do at home, so it was a nice change.

I also got to let off some steam with a boys trip to Vegas – it was a friend of a Tim's stag do, and you don't need asking twice when it comes to Vegas. Obviously under normal circumstances Amy would not have agreed to me going, but she is more than happy when she's in Laguna Beach and didn't mind me going at all. She also got to spend some time on her own with Tim's wife DeAnna and their twin nine month old boys William and Kenneth. The trip to Vegas was as you'd imagine - just nonstop drinking. I was amazed at my stamina, given the fact I hadn't drank anything for months and am not a big drinker anyway. But I was still there at 5am on the roof of Caesar's Palace having some tequila slammers for the road. I don't remember leaving or getting back to my hotel, but do remember trying to find my room in the 'Mandalay Bay' by putting my room card in every door in the corridor till a light went green. This is a risky manoeuvre in Vegas as you don't know who's in these rooms, a gangsta rapper's post show party could've been in full swing, with one of their entourage bursting out to pop a cap in my white ass.

All too soon the time came to go home and say goodbye to our friends. We hate leaving Laguna Beach – there's no hassle there, no stress - but you've got to go home at some point. So everything packed, we said good by to Southern California, blue skies and sunshine, heading back to the grey damp of 'Manch-Vegas'.

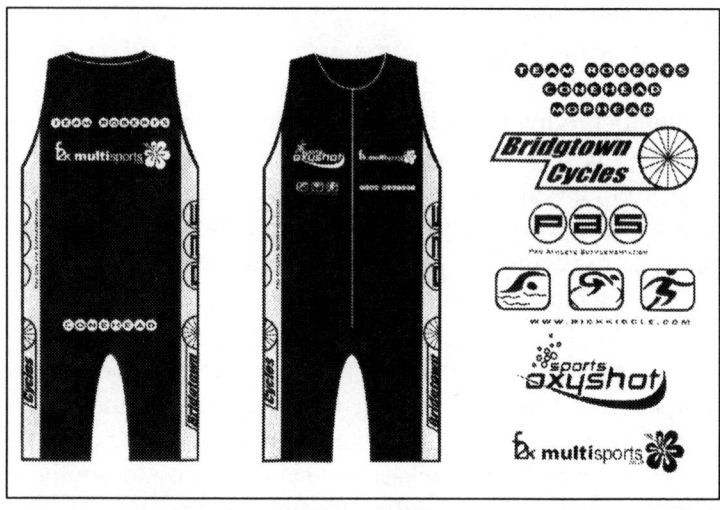

Team Roberts 2007 race kit and 'sponsors' – Despite being fat and slow I managed to blag these people into helping me. It's amazing how far sympathy and a case of Red Bull will go....

Ironman Switzerland 2007 – Another one bites the dust! I had a terrible race and horrific sunburn, but a finish is a finish.

Chapter 22

Beyond Ironman...

Returning to the UK meant returning to work, but not training. The bursar under my left Achilles tendon had flared up so I needed some more treatment from *City Physio* in Manchester City Centre. It was something that had started to come on before Ironman and was simply a result of the amount of training I was doing. But I hadn't kept on top of my flexibility work in my calves and even though the running wasn't that drastic on holiday it still brought it back on. So I had to lay off running again, but could still swim and do weights.

The first swim session was horrendous. If I needed a practical reminder of 'reversibility' this was a master class. I was like an asthmatic pensioner with brick like streamlining in the pool. I couldn't believe how much fitness I'd lost in the eight weeks since last swimming, which was race day. The weight sessions were equally as poor. Despite easing myself back into them during our trip to the US I was still as weak as a kitten. Regardless of this I had to think about my 2007 race plans and whether to do another Ironman or just concentrate on OD races. I was hooked though - as crazy as it sounds the place Ironman took me too mentally and physically was somewhere I wanted to get back to, somewhere I *needed* to get back to. I never thought I'd say that! It's such a 'pure' experience I wanted to get back to it, and be faster.

Work, as always, was up in the air as it came to the end of the year. Working in sport means you're only ever two steps away from being sacked and you're reliant on all sorts of other people and circumstances which dictate your future, none of which you have control over. Despite not really knowing what I was doing workwise and having no definite plans, I still had to think about a race in 2007. Speaking to a few people I was surprised to learn that they thought I'd struggle to get a decent race. Undeterred, I went onto *ironman.com* and began searching for a race. With my first long distance race out of the way on home soil it was now time to look overseas.

As an event I was unimpressed with Ironman UK - the ridiculous dual carriageway run, the wildly different con-centrations of energy drink at different aid stations and diet coke as opposed to normal coca-cola (yes, diet coke). I'd also had 'Ironweek' talked up to me by Ironman veterans but this was a non-thing at Ironman UK. This doesn't take anything away from the achievement of finishing an Ironman, but as an *'event'*, Ironman UK isn't great.

The next Ironman race had to incorporate a pay off for the family, so Ironman Oz and New Zealand sprung to mind immediately. Unfortunately both these races were in Spring, meaning I'd have to train through winter. Can you imagine doing a six hour ride in January? There isn't even six hours of daylight in January, so the Southern Hemisphere races were eliminated. What about the US? Ironman Florida seemed to have a good reputation, but the 2007 race had filled just days after entries had opened, as had Lake Placid and in Europe, Austria had also filled within days of entries opening. Arizona was still open but again that was in April, too early. Trying to find a race in a location I liked at the right time of year was proving to be easier said than done, I needed one some time in the summer or late summer.

I started looking at half distance races, Ironman 70.3. There was a great looking race in Southern California, just thirty minutes south of Laguna Beach, and another one in Hawaii, on the Island of Kona, not that it mattered to Amy which island we went to! But these seemed a long way to go do a 'half'. I'd done half distance in training, so I didn't see the point in all the expense and travelling to go and race what amounts to a very long training session. One race did seem to fit the bill – Ironman Switzerland in June 2007. It was in the centre of Zurich, was just two hours away by plane and looked stunning. Even though I wasn't exactly sure what the income situation was going to be in 2007, I decided I couldn't afford *not* to enter. Credit card out and bosh I was in Ironman Switzerland, the flights and hotel booked.

In a final act of Ironman madness I had the 'M-dot' tattoo on the inside of my left ankle. I'd booked it days after finishing the race but the tattooist, Loui Malloy, is booked up months in advance, meaning I had to wait three months. Loui is best known for his work on footballers and celebs, including David Beckham and I'd had a tattoo from him four years earlier. It was a fairly substantial thing in the small of my back, unusual because I'd waited till I was 30 years old to get one. Despite serving nine years in the forces I'd resisted all efforts and temptations to get a tattoo, including my para wings. I'd vowed not to get another tattoo as the 1½ hours of feeling like a blow torch in the small of my back wasn't something I wanted to repeat. Sitting there having the M-dot on my ankle was nowhere near as painful as actually doing the race, which was something I chatted with Loui about. He thought I was crazy, and maybe you do have to be a bit mental to do Ironman. Or is it more crazy not to? Besides, having the tattoo meant I didn't have to wear my finisher's top everywhere I went.

2007 saw the start of my training for Ironman Switzerland, but with a difference. It was all about quality rather than volume and this allowed for more family time and less stress. The psychological training demon which constantly told me I wasn't doing enough, I called the 'M-Dot' after the Ironman logo. But M-Dot doesn't have much of a voice these days and if I do find myself listening to it, it's usually worth listening to it because it is a session I actually have to do. The other difference in doing Switzerland is it's eight weeks earlier than IMUK.

Training plodded on, including selling the flat and moving to the 'burbs. We were a 'proper' family now with a detached house, large garden and more importantly a garage to store the bikes, wetsuits, supplements, pumps, spares, wheels! The 'blade didn't stay in the garage obviously, during the off season it sat on one of the wooden beams on the living room in the flat like a very expensive ornament. Moving to the new house meant the 'blade had a place of it's own – a heated, carpeted cupboard under the stairs. Is it wrong that I clean it with baby wipes? Amy asked if she should set a place at the dinner table for it...

The 'blade had also had some fettling over the winter. I'd dropped it off with Mike for a post winter service, and when the call came for me to pick it up, it wasn't the phone call I was expecting. They'd found a crack on the frame and it was being sent back to Trek, but ultimately it was terminal......the 'blade was dead! I was gutted, the bike that had carried me to Ironman glory was no more. Trek frames are guaranteed for life so the frame would be replaced, but even so it was sad to see the end of that 'blade. Basically the Bontrager carbon crank had caused problems where the front mech is, and they'd found a hairline crack. Mike had a frame ready to go and was just waiting for the nod from Trek when I got another unexpected call – the 'blade was not in fact dead.

Trek had put the camera down the seat tube and the hairline crack was just in the paintwork and not the frame. It was alive! Apparently this was a common problem with the carbon cranks, the fix was to fit an Ultegra chainset. Before I even had a chance to express how unhappy I was with having an Ultegra chainset on the 'blade, Mike went on to say he was going to fit a Dura-Ace chainset and absorb the extra cost! What a guy and what a shop. How's that for service?! The 'blade now had the Dura-Ace bling it deserved and whilst it was being upgraded I thought I might as well spend some money I didn't have on it.

It had traditional drop down road bars as opposed to aero/cow horn type bars with bar end shifters. I didn't like bar end shifters and unless you're an elite I think traditional STI's are more suitable for Ironman. But you can't put STI's on aero bars – unless you call Mike and task him with it! After spending a day trying different bars and set ups, he called me to tell me they'd managed it and it was ready to pick up. They didn't even charge me for the labour just the parts – a mere £90. I even adopted some race kit and officially formed 'Team Roberts', which was all a nonsense but it made me feel the part. Black and silver complete with Giro Aero Helmet for the shorter races, I had the carbon bike, the aero helmet, was shaved and the Ironman tattoo. It was over - I had turned completely to the dark side of triathlon geek-dom. The whole show is still run by Lilly-Mae though, she will always be team manager.

The new season started, the 'blade was released from its cupboard. A half distance race in 4 hours and 58 minutes. I even took part in some cycle races in an effort to improve the bike leg on IM, but cyclists are an even bigger bunch of oddballs than triathletes, especially when you get into the 100 mile cyclesportives. Then again, they all thought I was an idiot.

Ironman Switzerland was a totally different experience to IMUK. I felt bad about 'dissing' IMUK. It wasn't the race organisers fault, it was a crap event. Triathlon and Ironman is a totally different animal in Europe, over 100,000 people come to watch the big European races. With that comes big sponsorship money, which means much better value for money as a participant. Not only are the events themselves much larger, the stuff you get given is also substantial. Ironman Switzerland was nearly £70 cheaper than IMUK, but you got a great rucksack plus tonnes of other goodies.

The expo and event was twice the size of IMUK with a huge kiddies playground which was a lifesaver for Amy on race day to keep Lilly-Mae occupied. You also came past transition every lap on the bike and run, meaning plenty of support, rather than disappearing onto a dual carriageway for 2 hours.

I've said before I'll never do IMUK again and that's true, so I suppose I'm part of the problem of not making IM a success in the UK. But it's investment from big sponsors that's needed, as well as a decent 'event' and course to run it on. It's a real eye opener to see how Ironman should be when you venture outside the UK.

As for the race itself, I had a terrible swim (1hr 18 minutes), an OK bike (6hrs 18 minutes) and a terrible run (4hrs 49 minutes). I scraped across the line in 12 hours 36 minutes, another '12 hour' finish but not the sub 12 hours I was hoping for. The 29° heat was a killer and Ironman is unpredictable – you're not going to run your perfect race every time. So I was disappointed but grateful to finish it, crossing the line with Lilly-Mae rather than in the back of an ambulance suffering heat exhaustion.

I did a much better job with the race nutrition though and by this time had discovered SiS 'go' gels, which were a revelation for me. I'd avoided using anything other than Powerbar as that's what's available on Ironman. But a top tip from a seasoned Ironman athlete was to fill a water bottle with as many gels as you'd need on the bike rather than grabbing them at feed stations. This had two main benefits, firstly you didn't have to piss about opening them with your teeth on the bike and secondly you could use your own choice of gel. PowerBar gels are great, but it's like eating wall paper paste and you have to consume plenty of water with them. The SiS gels on the other hand are isotonic (no water needed) and have a thin watery texture with just a hint of flavour. This meant I didn't get sick of them on the bike and can still look at one now without throwing up.

Chapter 23

What's with the book...?

The writing of this book was a key part of finishing off the Ironman experience. As I mentioned in the foreword, I liked the idea of having a book out there on Ironman that was just about the training and race story from someone having a go at it, not a technical training manual. Maybe there's a tip in here that could prove useful. If something technical helps someone in any way then I've exceeded my own expectations of this book.

I want people to realise that Ironman is not an impossible task reserved for the uber fit, and despite my vocational knowledge I was as amateur as any first timer. The point being there is no advantage to be had when training for an Ironman, no shortcut. Doesn't matter what you know, what you think you know, how fit you are or are not. Come race day it's down to you and you alone.

The unforeseen benefit of doing this was the therapeutic experience. To put the journey into words means that I know exactly why I did Ironman and what I went through doing it, no chance to gloss over anything with the rose tint of time during the weeks and months after the race. It would be easy to just remember the sense of achievement, avoiding the difficult questions that got asked in the dark corners of my mind and how I responded to them.

There's also an element of vanity in this, to have something else to show for all the training (and pain!!) from the race itself. When Lilly-Mae grows up I want her to have more than just dusty photos and some medals combined with my vague memory to understand the Ironman experience, and me too. When I'm too old to do anything, and have adopted a tartan blanket of my own I can bore people's tits off with this book.

I suppose the only thing I haven't talked about is the financial cost, and I was going to use this as the final tot up, having only started triathlon with a sprint in May 2006 and the Ironman just three months later. But you know – who cares what it actually cost and continues to cost? I have an accountant that counts my beans for me, and regardless of how much it cost, it was worth every penny.

One last thing, mind the bears…!

Lightning Source UK Ltd.
Milton Keynes UK
29 October 2010

162048UK00011B/4/A